CW01649126

People I Met on the Way

Fifty Years a Priest in Brazil

by

Father Joseph Dillon SVD

Edited by Maura McRobbie

The rights of Joseph Dillon to be identified as the author of this work have been asserted.

Maura McRobbie asserts the moral right to be identified as the editor and compiler of this work.

No part of this publication may be reproduced or transmitted in any form or by any means electronic, digital, including photocopying, recording or any storage information system, without prior written permission from the publisher.

This book should not be sold, resold, lent or circulated in any forms of binding or cover, other than which it is printed presently, without the prior written consent of the publisher.

ISBN Number 978-1-7396638-1-0

Published by MMCR Independent
© 2023

For further information,
www.mauramcrobbie.com

Reviews

"A wonderful insight into a lifelong ministry. A very readable and enjoyable memoir."

Father Joseph Mackle, Parish Priest, St Andrew's RC church, Bearsden

"Father Joseph's life of creative, courageous, and compassionate engagement with the people of Brazil is a story of liberative faith and hope against all the odds. An eye-opening, inspiring call to action and change!"

Father John Riches, Anglican Priest, St Mary's Episcopalian Cathedral, Glasgow. Former Professor of Divinity and Biblical Criticism at the University of Glasgow.

"Father Joseph's readiness to be involved in community life in various parishes encouraged many people to become involved too in local programmes and learning.

This account of a life well lived should be shared with young people in our secondary schools and diocesan youth groups. Father Joe is a wonderful role model."

Rana Keane, Former Education Adviser, Diocese of Paisley

INTRODUCTION

I am very pleased to have undertaken the role of publishing and editing this memoir. I had heard stories about Padre Jose Dillon through my childhood, growing up in the late 1960s. My paternal grandmother, Florence, was his mother's sister. Although my grandmother lived in Glasgow in Scotland, Jose's mother Mollie, lived in Dublin and they were great letter-writers. She filled my grandmother in on all the details of her youngest son, leaving Dublin to become a Divine Word priest. I remember my grandmother recounting the joy of his ordination in Donamon in Ireland in 1972 and then the sadness of his mother as she waved farewell to him as he embarked on his career as a missionary priest in Brazil. This was in 1973.

Now in 2023, Jose has been 50 years a priest in Brazil and in this memoir, he recounts his working life in the communities of Sao Paulo during the military regime of the 1980s through to the Bolsonaro presidency of more recent times. He describes his work with the indigenous communities of the Amazon, where he helped to empower the lives of those in the remotest areas to have access to

better health and educational opportunities. In the favelas of Sao Paulo he details the challenges he faced, witnessing senseless murders and drug-fuelled crimes, and yet, he has set up health projects in parish communities, bringing herbal remedies and hope to the thousands of people who live in these lawless communities, longing for a more peaceful, productive way of life.

This memoir, 'People I Met on The Way', is not simply about people and their daily activities, it is about Brazil, the largest country in Latin America and the rich layer upon layer of civilisations that have lived on this land since records began. It is about the lives and cultures of the indigenous people who were enslaved by the Portuguese and Spanish, and then evangelised by Christian missionaries. It is about multiracial 20th century Brazil with a history of receiving immigrants to work in the plantations once slavery was abolished, leaving too their footprints on the landscape. It is about the 21st century Brazil, with a new president, a new hope for the planet and the people of Brazil.

Maura McRobbie
February 2023

PREFACE

This is my memoir of 50 years as a missionary priest in Brazil, from 1973 until 2023. When I was newly ordained, I was sending letters home to my mother in Dublin. Sometimes I'd be going through difficult situations, but I'd keep these from her to prevent her from worrying. Instead I would tell her about the people, the priests and the parishes, keeping her entertained with lots of details and funny stories.

Writing handwritten letters was the norm then, it was an enjoyable way to spend an evening, and letters would take about a fortnight to arrive and a further fortnight for a reply. In those days there seemed to be far more time. Now, with emails and laptops, writing is equally enjoyable, but seems to be carried out in far more haste and with a lot more urgency. Replies come instantly, and there is less time for thought and reflection.

However, as a result of the coronavirus pandemic in 2020, there was plenty of time for reflection, and as my memories flickered through my mind, often jogged by photographs of familiar faces and events,

I knew that it was somehow the perfect time, to set out my story, my memoir, for you dear readers to enjoy.

I wish to thank all the parishioners I have worked with along the way, many of whom have become dear friends, and have helped me to become a deeper, more humble follower of Christ. I would like to thank my sisters Julie and Mary, who corrected my original first draft (written in Portuguese and translated into English).

I am deeply indebted and enormously grateful to Maura McRobbie. The work she has undertaken for this publication in English has been substantial, moving deftly between my original manuscripts, photographs and so many narratives and stories from across the years. She has assembled this material and given it the flow and rhythm it now possesses. Thank you again Maura, for being my publisher and editor as I take my first steps into the world of writing.

Father Joseph Dillon
SVD (Divine Word Missionary)
February 2023

Map of Brazil

CONTENTS

CHAPTER 1

Three Cows and a Shovel

Facing retirement, I often wondered what would give my life more meaning and purpose. It's the same question I faced in my youth, when I wondered what career path I'd follow, and whether I'd marry and have a family or whether I'd stay at home with my mother as the eternal Irish bachelor. It's strange that a significant transition in life, calls to mind another transition: from teenager to man; from parish priest to retired priest. I had always imagined that I'd die actively in service in a parish, so facing a life beyond the parish has left me somewhat ill at ease.

After visiting a nursing home in Germany on a trip home to Europe in 2019, I realised that I needed something transformational to keep me from ending up in a nursing or care home. It was as I concelebrated mass for retired missionaries of the Sister Servants of the Holy Spirit (SSpS) in Laupheim near Stuttgart, where I had worked as a young man in the 1970s, that I felt overcome with an urge to find something that would keep me active and purposeful until the day I died. I watched all these elderly sisters struggle bravely in wheelchairs and walking aids and remembered how lively and enthusiastic they had once been.

Strangely, on this same trip to Germany, in Wetzlar, close to Frankfurt, I had been asked to dinner at a friend's home. These friends were older now, but in the early 1970s when I was training to be a priest, they had inspired me on my spiritual journey. They had followed my missionary work in Brazil with interest, and their daughter Brigitta, now a dentist and her husband Sven, wanted to hear about my life there. They lived in the country with Sven's grandfather Karl who was 98. At dinner Karl asked me all about President Bolsonaro, who he knew was very unpopular in Germany. His knowledge of the political situation in Brazil impressed me, and I was amazed when not long after dinner, he excused himself from the table saying he had work to do.

I later asked the family what his work was. I noticed that he had no mobility issues, no curvature of the spine, no memory issues or Alzheimer's, and his mind was as sharp as a tack. Sven, his grandson took me out to the barn, and there I found Karl, cheerfully forking grass to feed three large cows, before going round behind them to shovel up the manure, which he collected before spreading it to fertilise outdoor crops.

"It's my hobby!" smiled Karl. "It keeps me fit."

If a hobby has this effect, I thought, I badly needed to find one too.

Before Brazil it was The Word that gave me a window on the world. It was a weekly magazine published by the Divine Word Missionaries that came into our house each week. It was the content and the context of The Word that really made an impact on me. The stories of the missionaries caught my imagination, communicating the joy they felt when helping those less fortunate than themselves. They had found their purpose in life.

At the age of sixteen I was asked to promote and help sell copies of The Word through the Legion of Mary in our parish of St Anthony's on Clontarf Road in Dublin. I was quite good at selling these and as a result, the confidence in my sales ability increased and I became a sales assistant in Arnotts in Henry Street for six years. The manager was impressed with my experience and my willingness in urging people to buy things, and I must say, I enjoyed working in wholesale where I met many buyers from the country towns in Ireland. However, I knew that it wasn't my main mission in life. During this time, I also organised youth dances in the parish with my friends John, Dick and Noel. We chose the music and helped to entertain the guests every Friday and Sunday night. From these dances many weddings came about. At this time, our lives were an empty canvas, waiting for the paint to be applied. Or perhaps as I like to think, we were on the foothills of the mountain range.

My hobby in my youth was mountain climbing. I wanted to climb as many as I could. And I suppose it was the mountains that led me to Donamon Castle in Roscommon and my first missionary steps. On vacation in Salzburg in Austria with my two friends, Noel and Arthur, we were going to climb Grosse Glockner (3978m) when we met some girls in the Youth Hostel we were staying at. We talked about everything, politics, religion, but no one tackled the third subject – sex. The girl I was talking to was Dutch, and with my interest in Catholic literature (ie, The Word) and working with the Legion of Mary, I promised that I would send her some Catholic magazines or books in Dutch. When I returned home to Dublin, our neighbour, directed me to the Divine Word Missionaries (SVD), that was founded in Holland. I wrote to the SVD in Roscommon and told them that I was looking for Dutch Catholic literature to send to a friend. I also told them about my interest in the work of the missionaries and that I was keen to do something that would make a difference to people in poorer countries. They invited me down to Donamon, their seminary, and to cut a long story short, I never sent the books or magazines to the Dutch girl, but I ended up joining the SVD.

I entered the seminary on August 15th the Feast of the Assumption, 1966. It was the year when the Church was being presented with changes brought about by Vatican II. I remember being told to bring with me a bible and a copy of Vatican Council Documents II. I asked my mother to buy a bible, and she unwittingly bought the Protestant St James' version. It didn't have the books written in Greek which is known as 'apocrypha', but neither of us would have known the difference at the time. I was 23, and over the next seven years I would learn how to become a missionary priest. Twenty of us started in our year group, and nine of us were ordained in December 1972. The lads that left, remained in touch with the SVD and I have many memories (some good and some not so good) of *playing* football with the guys, something I'd never done before. At school it was hockey or hurling I had played.

During the holidays as a seminarian, I worked in old people's care homes. These were managed by nuns and I knew that I was helping to give them some respite by volunteering to work over the summer months. On my first day, one of the old people came enthusiastically to greet me, shaking my hand vigorously. I was impressed by the warm welcome I was given, only to find that when my hand was released, it was covered in this old fellow's excrement. No matter how many times I scrubbed my hands that evening, I couldn't rid myself of the smell. I felt that I couldn't go back to the home. I couldn't sleep and was rehearsing my excuses to the sisters, but somehow, when I offered the experience to Christ in prayer, when I let go of myself, and looked for Christ in all the old people, I found a way to go back and be of use, allowing the sisters who worked there tirelessly day and night, to have their holidays. I suppose that helped give me a sense of purpose, supporting others.

One summer I went to London to work as an orderly in Mile End Hospital. My job was to take the patients by trolley into the theatre and wait for them to be returned to the ward. As well as the various types of operations, abortions were also being carried out. I could see from the patients' hospital notes the reason for their abortions. One day the nurse in charge of the operating theatre asked me what I was doing working with abortion patients, surely as a missionary, this was against Catholic values? I sent a letter to the novice master at the seminary seeking his advice. He replied that as an orderly I wasn't directly involved, only the surgeon, the anaesthetist and the scrub nurse were participating, and it was a matter for their consciences, not mine.

The next year I went back to working with the elderly in a War Veteran's hospital in London. In one geriatric ward I looked after an old man who had lost his legs in World War 1. He had been in bed, immobile, for fifty years. At another hospital, St Olave's in Rotherhithe. I learned from the charge nurse, how to care for the elderly in this area, many of whom were retired dockers who had led hard lives and were impatient and used very coarse language in their suffering. This nurse taught me how to respect and treat their wounds and complaints with patience and kindness. It was in this hospital that I met a student nurse Joanne who was to become a lifelong friend.

I feel I was always meant to work with old people as I made great friends with an old lady Ellie Larkin, as a seminarian in Roscommon. I would visit her when my spirits were low or I didn't feel like studying. She always had the kettle on over the fire, and a cup of tea ready. I visited other old people on my bicycle and I organised parties and days out for them at the seminary. It was a great pleasure to see Ellie Larkin at my first mass, in the Sacred Heart Home for the elderly in Roscommon after I was ordained. I didn't realise then that nine months later I would be heading for Brazil. I had found my purpose.

CHAPTER 2

It's a Hard Life

I arrived in Brazil on the 12th October 1973, on the feast day of Our Lady of the Americas (Nossa Senhora Aparecida). It was Margarita Maria Schwade a Brazilian nun known as Sister Ursula who encouraged me to choose Brazil while studying at the seminary in Ireland. She talked about the culture, the climate, the language and the type of work missionaries were doing there. She understood the nature of South America and its political precariousness. Previously I had considered South Africa, and was interested in its struggle against Apartheid, but I felt that eventually European missionaries would be expelled from almost all of Africa as a result of its colonial past. In Asia I felt I would find it difficult to fit in, that I would always be an outsider, whereas there was something about South America that I related to, but what, I wasn't quite sure.

I knew I wanted to work with the poor and the oppressed, I didn't want to work in schools and I wanted to work in areas where Christianity offered a way of transforming lives. In Argentina, at this time, where many Europeans had settled, I felt there was less need for evangelization, and in Paraguay I would have been required to learn native Guarani as well as Spanish. Mexico was also Spanish-speaking, but I would have needed to work within the school system and this was not where I felt my strengths lay, so instead I began to do research into Brazil. The evenings spent with Sister Ursula drinking copious cups of tea in the seminary provided me with the information I required. I learned that almost all of South America was under military governments, some more cruel than others, and that Brazil had been under a military regime since 1964. It was interesting to hear how the Church and the people were coping.

I was impressed with the work of the bishops there, especially Archbishop Helder Câmara. (1909 – 1999) He was an advocate of Liberation Theology (LT) an approach that emphasised the liberation of the poor through the teachings of the gospel in communities, leading them to achieve a more dignified and proactive way of life. Câmara was a significant force in challenging the military regime. He was quoted as saying,

"When I give food to the poor, they call me a saint. When I ask why they are poor, they call me a communist."

In my research, I also discovered that the Vatican Council documents were being translated into Portuguese and Spanish in Medellin in Colombia in 1968. These were pivotal to the future direction of the Catholic church in South America. Its key message was to support a preferential option for the poor and to "defend the cause of the weak and fatherless; maintain the rights of the poor and oppressed. Rescue the weak and needy; deliver them from the hand of the wicked." It also encouraged the Church to "form national communities that reflected a global organization, where all of the peoples but more especially the lower classes played an active role in the construction of a new society." The participation of the Brazilian Bishops and the Vatican council documents were very influential in my decision to go to South America, but where exactly in Brazil? I learned that there was a strong German influence in the southern province, and in the northern province schools were the priority, so I decided on the central province which had different types of pastoral and parish work that would suit my wish to work with the poor and oppressed.

As I settled into my Swiss Air flight from Frankfurt Airport to Galeão Airport in Rio de Janeiro, I wasn't prepared for the pilot's announcement that there had been a military coup in Chile and it might be wiser for passengers travelling to Santiago in Chile to disembark at Rio de Janeiro. As I was later to learn, the military coup, backed by the American government, had bombed the Palacio de La Moneda and the Socialist leader, Salvador Allende, committed suicide before he could be arrested. Thus began the military dictatorship of General Augusto Pinochet in Chile which lasted 17 years. This was to become as equally brutal and intolerant as the regime I was entering in Brazil. Backed again by the US government and a Conservative Catholic church, it served as a model for other Latin American countries to adopt as a way of developing nationalism, economic development and anti-communism. I have since spoken to people over the years in Brazil who feel that these dictatorships were a good thing, because some people '*made fortunes*' and prospered. However, subsequent democratically chosen socialist governments have shown that a better distribution of wealth is possible.

Arriving at the airport, it had been arranged that I would be met by Father Silvestre who would be my SVD guide. I didn't expect to be met by the military police armed with machine guns. When I was asked what my profession was, I stumbled with my pronunciation of Padre (priest) – and said Pé meaning 'a foot' in Portuguese. Luckily, Father Silvestre was waiting for me in the crowd and he came to my rescue, explaining I was the new missionary priest. Silvestre had driven the hundreds of kilometres from Sao Paulo to Rio to meet me. I thought Sao Paulo was a forty-minute drive from Rio de Janeiro, but in fact it was 6 hours away, a 464km distance. Drenched in sweat, his colleague, Paulo Evers, a financial advisor to SVD who was with him, suggested we stop for lunch. He told me that while we have a vow of poverty this doesn't mean that we are miserable. I have considered this frequently in my fifty years as I have witnessed so many celebrations and festivities. During my first Brazilian barbecue (churrasco) with Father Sylvestre and Paulo on that day, I was amazed to see huge skewers of barbecued beef, piping hot from the red brick open fires, being served, the size of which I had never seen in Ireland. From the hilltop of the open-air barbecue, we could see the construction site of the Basilica Nossa Senhora Aparecida. in the distance. I didn't know then that this would later be the name of my parish from 1989 – 2005. This Basilica would be visited by three popes over the next forty years: Pope John Paul II in 1980; Pope Benedict in 2007 and Pope Francis in 2013.

Father Silvestre was a great guide to me in those early days. He advised me to stay in the minor seminary of Araraquara in the state of Sao Paulo. Here I could spend time learning Portuguese. I had taped some lessons before leaving Ireland and I would walk around the football pitch repeating phrases out loud tirelessly, perfecting my pronunciation and accent. At mealtimes in the refectory, I would try these out with the priests, who would laugh as I entertained them with my less than proficient Portuguese.

I attended an SVD evening school (Duque de Caxias) but I found that the other students only wanted to try out their English on me. They would lose interest in their teacher and joke around with me. I was embarrassed that I was such a source of fascination to them. In addition, in this initial year, I joined five different Portuguese classes and everyone invited me to their end of the year parties. I was beginning to think (what I was not feeling,) – 'what a hard life it was to be a missionary!!!' One teacher, Mercedes came to the seminary every day and she really helped me to speak and understand Portuguese. She also gave me guidance on social situations and preparing homilies for the daily mass I was saying in a local care home. Nuns ran this care home and after mass I would anxiously ask the sisters if the elderly had understood my Portuguese. I would then be told that most of them were deaf and the rest were only there waiting for breakfast to be served, so it didn't make much difference whether my Portuguese was coherent or not. This did wonders for my self-esteem, but each day Mercedes continued to correct my grammar and encourage my pronunciation until I was word perfect. She also tutored me on how to read and write the Brazilian road signs for the highway code as I required a driver's license. There was a written exam and I passed with 100%, while many others struggled. It was Mercedes' patient tuition that got me there, and I thank her to this day. Sadly, Mercedes died much too young from cancer a few years later but I have never forgotten her patience and willingness to ensure that I learned my Portuguese correctly. May she rest in peace.

Another teacher I had at this time was Dirce. She was different from Mercedes in that as she corrected my Portuguese, I corrected her

English! We had a love hate relationship with language, but she gave me a magnificent dictionary in 1974 that I still use to this day.

The following year, Father Sylvestre and some members of the SVD, travelled once again to the airport, this time to Viracopas in Campinas to meet Mick MacGuiness, a colleague from our class in Ireland. He was to become a great friend and it was during this car journey that Father Sylvestre told us we would be both going to study in Rio de Janeiro at the Centro de Formação Intercultural (CENFI) on the language and culture of Brazil.

CHAPTER 3

Rio, Rock and Roll and Registro

Our first day in Rio de Janeiro in February 1974 was marked by the news of a terrible tragedy in Sao Paulo where we had just left. A high-rise building called Joelma in downtown São Paulo, had gone on fire killing 187 people, and leaving more than 300 injured. There was an outpouring of grief among the people as we left. We arrived at the Carmelite Convent of Santa Teresa where the centre we were to study at was located. We had travelled there by tram, and I learned that the road of the convent led to the Corcovado, which is the mountain where the figure of Christ the Redeemer stands. We visited this many times as it was on our doorstep and each time it was the most amazing, awe-inspiring view.

However, we were not far from the favelas which provided another glimpse of the Brazilian way of life. One of the Carmelite nuns asked me to do a weekly mass at the nearby favela of Morro dos Prazeres (Hill of Pleasures) and I accepted. Although it was called Hill of Pleasures, and was named as a tribute to a nun, Mother Maria dos Prazeres, who held mass at the bottom of the hill several years before, it was certainly not a pleasurable place to be. The living conditions were dire with houses made of flimsy plywood piled one on top of each other on stilts, stacked against the hillside. One of the families invited me for dinner after mass one Sunday. The traditional stew being served was typically Brazilian, a Feijoada, made with black beans and pork. Unfortunately, my first mouthful was a piece of pig's ear. No matter how hard I chewed, I could not break it down, and not wanting to offend the host by spitting it out, I distracted her by asking for salt. As she went into the kitchen, I removed the pig's ear from my mouth and squeezed it through one of the gaps in the floorboards where the pigs below rushed to devour it. I have never since been able to eat a Brazilian Feijoada.

During this time, the main cause of violence and aggression in the favela was drink. Now it is drugs related. On a Sunday morning when I was saying mass, it had a fairly peaceful ambience, but at night it was full of crime. Today this favela, Morro dos Prazeres is one of the most violent places in Rio with two visitors recently being murdered at gunpoint when they wandered accidently off the tourist track.

Another course participant was a French-Canadian sister whose name was Monica. She invited Mick and I to visit where she worked in Minas Gerais. This is a state in south-east Brazil that produces coffee and is famed for its architecture that is steeped in its colonial past. Monica lived in a town called Mozartlandia and as we travelled there, we noticed the magnificent landscape with mountains, waterfalls, valleys and large areas of fertile lands. We went horse-riding with Monica and had barbecues with friends in her community. The Carnival in February was also a highlight of our stay in Rio, and I had enjoyed the one in Sao Paulo the year before, and every year since. The world famed Leblon Beach was on our doorstep, and we discovered that it was one of the cheapest ways to live. On our days off, we would go for beach walks, a sunbathe and a swim. In the evenings one of our favourite haunts was Bob's Burgers in Rio for an ice cream soda. Sister Frances Baker was also in our group, and we each knew that we only had a few short months to live and enjoy Rio before we took up our missionary posts. I learned so many things in these months: the joy of new friendships and discovering a new culture and experiences together. I also learned that I definitely didn't have samba in my blood – but I definitely had rock and roll.

Mick and I were invited to visit a Divine Word parish in Brasilia. Brasilia was founded in 1960 to serve as the new capital of Brazil. It was awarded World Heritage Status by UNESCO in 1987 due to its modernist architecture, but I didn't like it at all. There were plenty of remarkable buildings, but they were shiny and soulless, and I felt the city was made for cars, and not for people. On my first day, I went for a walk into town looking for a shop or a store that sold cans of coke or soft drinks, but after walking for a kilometre in the baking heat, I couldn't find anything. I returned to the parish and decided to try my first beer from a large stock that was in the freezer. Beer was never my drink of choice, but in the name of thirst, I drank my first beer. The parish had planned to hold a festival that week, but due to heavy rains, it had to be cancelled. This meant that there was plenty of beer for me to quench my thirst!

Not long after this trip, our course in Rio was complete, and Mick and I had to return to the seminary in Araraquara. We had an old beat-up car and as we drove the 474 km distance, neither of us remembered to put oil in the engine. The next day when we started the car, the engine had melted. Notwithstanding this negligence, Mick was appointed to a parish in Araraquara to work with young people, and I was transferred to the city of Sao Paulo to a parish named Cristo Rei (Christ the King).

Father Candido Falqueto was the parish priest and together with Father Joao Laub, I became part of the team. Many priests from the Divine Word passed through Cristo Rei. One of them was Father José Morshauser who was well known in the area for his healing and many came to him to be cured of their illnesses. He was an enigmatic figure dressed in a black cassock and wearing dark glasses. He spoke with a strong accent and he sucked ice cubes for his throat. He met with the people individually at the back of the church and long queues would soon appear when he was there. I took the opportunity to practise my Portuguese with those in the queue, asking them about the bible, or the sacraments or anything to do with mass. I think it was more of a trial for them than the illnesses they had, but they were too polite to say. I always wondered too if Father José's cures were effective.

On Monday everyone disappeared from the parish and I was alone, so I would take the bus into Avenida Celso Garcia to the cinema where usually two films were shown along with a trailer. I also became a frequent visitor to the Municipal Theatre, which was also a concert venue on Monday evenings where I became a fan of Chopin. I became friendly with the Irish Sisters of the Holy Rosary in their parish at Quarto Centenário of São Paulo. I didn't realise then that I would return to work here twenty-five years later in 1998. They introduced me to many of the Irish priests who worked in the congregations of the Holy Spirit in Vila Alpina. I played tennis with Father George Boran who was the coordinator of the Youth of Sao Paulo. He helped me to organise youth groups in the neighbourhood of Tatuapé, and at this time, youth groups were a large and strong movement within the church.

I remember these young people as optimistic, full of energy and enthusiastic for the future. We organised special youth masses and they participated fully in these. We held meetings that explored the new Vatican II theology and the value of sharing. The Campaigns of Fraternity and sharing bread together were the themes of our meetings and I had my first adult baptism as a result of the Youth Group.

In 1975, the SVD transferred the parish over to the Diocese and Father Candido went to St Marcos in the outskirts of Sao Paulo, and I was sent southwards to the city of Registro on the Atlantic coast, 168 km from São Paulo. In the mid-17th century, the first gold deposits in Portuguese America were discovered in this region. The Portuguese Crown registered the gold which resulted in the emergence of a town, called Registro, before it was shipped to Europe. By the end of the 17th century, gold mining terminated with the discovery of better mines in neighbouring Minas Gerais and Goiás, and many of the miners from this area emigrated, leaving the mining activity in relative neglect. However, much of the architecture and decaying grandeur of times past, remained in Registro when I arrived.

CHAPTER 4

Weddings, Wakes and Wisdom

The bus journey to Registro seemed to take an eternity. I was a real novice among the established Dutch priests, all SVD's: and the main one being Father Warenhoven. They had strong opinions and were very present and connected with their parishioners. There was a young parish secretary named Irani who worked there until she left to be an administrator in the law. However, she later became a missionary herself, and married a missionary and now lives with her family in Sao Paulo.

I began working with the elderly, many of whom needed all kinds of assistance. Sister Elizabeth (Beth) was a nurse in the local clinic and she really encouraged my pastoral work. Beth was from Austria and on trips back to Europe, I climbed mountains in Austria with members of her family. She later left Registro for Rubim in Minas Gerais, then went on to Amapa at the mouth of the Amazon River, before returning to Sao Paulo.

The inhabitants of the coastal area of Registro are called Caiçaras and are made up of indigenous people, European settlers and former

African slaves. For at least three hundred years, the Caiçaras lived on fishing and farming in one of the most beautiful unspoiled areas of the Atlantic Coast. However, in the late 1970s, a huge motorway was built, the BR101 and opened the door to massive tourism with real estate speculation damaging the indigenous way of life. During the time I was there, it was still virtually unspoilt, and I found the people in the city and in the more rural areas to be both reserved and respectful.

The River Ribeira de Iguape runs through Registro and upriver many of the communities could only be reached by canoe. Many of the families lived in makeshift houses, and many were extremely poor. The only way to visit them was to leave the car and go upriver by one of these simple boats. On other occasions, when I went to say mass in the interior region, I found I needed to trek two hours by foot until I reached the chapel locations. These chapels were also makeshift shelters, usually made with straw roofs and without walls. Once when I was saying mass, just as I was raising the host at the consecration, I could see a huge 'caninana' entwined in the beams and basking in the heat of the candles. In those early days, I didn't know the difference between a harmless snake and a poisonous one. Fortunately, some members of the congregation got it down easily with sticks and they reassured me that it was harmless. They let it go and told me that the 'caninana' was excellent for dealing with rodents. Despite its reputation as being a wild snake, it was not dangerous, even although it could reach 2.5 metres in length and was very quick and agile.

Back in the city, I had started bible courses for the youth groups of the parish. This was a good way of getting to know people and to see how they interpreted the various texts of the bible. We would explore the Old and New Testament and many of the group members became 'leaders' and they were able to deliver the bible study groups into the communities, spreading the word and keeping in weekly contact with those living outwith the city. Often, the leaders in Registro were future university students with huge amounts of energy and enthusiasm. My role was to fill the van each week (the parish had an old blue VW camper van we called Kombi) and drop them off at locations all over the rural areas. On the return journeys there was always plenty of laughter and things to discuss. We'd end our meetings by planning what we would do next time, and within months, the 'city' leaders had managed to train and identify 'rural' leaders to continue spreading the word.

The youth groups were adventurous and full of ideas. They created a 50km challenge walk from Registro to Eldorado and while there was plenty of objections from the older members of the parish and the older priests (it's too far; it's a crazy idea; they'll die of heatstroke;) I supported them and worked with them to make it a success. We arranged to meet up with other communities along the way for food and refreshments and to stay overnight at one of these locations. And armed with plenty of water, prayers and full of the spirit, it turned out to be an unforgettable fun event.

The religious characters I met in Registro were unforgettable too: Sister Arnaldia, a retired German lady who had been a mathematician. She taught the gospels through maths and algebra. Sister Beth and Misae too, were wonderful teachers, teaching what they knew about Christ and sharing their knowledge with others. However, it was in Registro that I learned how 'excluding' and indeed off-putting Catholicism can be. For example, I could only baptize children of married parents. Godparents too had to be practising Catholics, or known within the parish, and as it was costly to get married, many new mothers with babies were single and I was not allowed to baptise them. I found this a very harsh interpretation of the teachings of Christ.

In an area called Bamburral, I had worked with a young leader, a Catechist, who had worked with all the First Communion children. On the day of their First Communion, she didn't turn up. I waited for her a while, but I was then told that she had run away to get married. Her family were so poor they were unable to provide a wedding reception party for the whole community and this would be frowned on. She was so ashamed, she chose to run away.

Superstition too was part of the daily life of the parish. One day a lady came into the church asking me if she could kiss the key to the tabernacle. I asked her why and she told me her partner was in prison, she had had a vision, that by kissing the key of the tabernacle, the doors of the prison would be opened. I knew her partner and I knew that he had stolen something, so I spoke to the judge dealing with his case, and yes, he was due to be released, but he had no papers, no formal ID card or documentation. So I wrote to the parish where he was born, and they forwarded me his baptism certificate. They also had her baptism certificate too, and with these, the judge was satisfied that he could be released. Before doing so, I was asked to marry them in jail, and a civil marriage took place later with the deputy mayor as bestman, and the judge as the official overseeing the marriage. Soon after, his delighted wife came to me and said:

"You see father......it was kissing the key of the tabernacle, and God did the rest!" Faith is like that you know!

There were a few frightening experiences too when I really thought my time had come. One evening I had a camper van full of young bible leaders and we were making our way upriver to one of the remote communities called Guaviruva. We had to cross the river, and usually the little wooden bridge was high above the water level. On this occasion, after heavy flooding, the bridge was well below the water line. I knew I should have stopped and turned back, but something in me made me put my foot hard onto the pedal and make a run at it. Immediately the headlamps were beneath the water and everything went dark. We made it just and no more, but that night I was traumatised by nightmares of me causing the drowning of several members of the community in our beloved Kombi van on our mission to spread the word of God.

It was in Guaviruva that Sister Misae encouraged me to bring some LP records and a record player to play at one of the youth groups. Singing the songs of Padre Zezhino was a way to communicate with the younger people. I tried my best, but I felt my Portuguese was letting me down. Sister Misae assured me that it was not my Portuguese or the music, it was just the young people were innately shy and withdrawn. I remember a young girl Cida here celebrating her 15th birthday. I was to meet Cida again later, this time she would be known as Nina.

In Bamburral at a funeral wake, after I had celebrated mass, I met an official from the Department of Political and Social Order. (DOPS) Unwittingly I said,

"Oh, is that not the department that tortures people?" His eyes stared back at me hard and he took his right arm and wrapped it round my throat from behind my shoulders. He squeezed my neck hard and said to me:

"Don't think if you end up at the DOPS that you can call your Bishop and you'll be let you off the hook. Because everyone that enters the DOPS is guilty, and no matter how many times you try to prove your innocence, we will prove the opposite. You will not come out alive."

I was shaken and I have no doubt that if this is how he treated a priest, how would he have treated a lay person who entered that hell? This was during the Military Regime of 1964 to 1985, and the person responsible for managing the DOPS at the time was Colonel Carlos Alberto Brilhante Ustra. He was convicted of crimes of torture and the National Truth Committee (CNV) recorded 45 deaths and more than 500 people were tortured in the basement of the DOPS. In recent times, Brazil's President Bolsonaro praised Colonel Carlos as a "national hero". As Samuel Johnson said in the late 18th century,

"Patriotism is the last refuge of the scoundrel" and "alleged patriotism, in all ages and countries, have been used as a cloak for their own interests."

Finally, it was in Registro that I learned a very important lesson in humility. It was during one of my first Sunday masses in a coastal community, where I was full of spiritual knowledge and wisdom that I wanted to impart to the Caiçaras. I must admit to a slight feeling of superiority as I entered the makeshift chapel with my vestments, chalice and scriptures. I felt like a foreigner abroad as I arrived, ready to give my sermon on the mount, even though I had little experience or pastoral insights. I just wanted to be listened to. However, halfway through the mass, I leaned over the altar and the candles set my vestment on fire. Rather than admitting what a fool I was, I tried to cover it up with my book of scriptures, but the smell of burning and the flames took hold and I was left coughing and spluttering in front of the assembled, dumbfounded congregation. Finally, when I got the flames out, I didn't even have the wit to laugh or make a joke. I carried on with the mass solemnly and tried to cover the large hole in my robe as best I could. Back in the sacristy I tore off my robe to see the damage. What an idiot I had been. These people would be laughing at me behind my back. I was mortified. But I learned that day in the chapel of Riberao Vermehlo the necessity to be able to laugh at oneself; to admit defeat; simplicity, humility and to walk in the footsteps of Christ.

A few years later, Father Warenhoven in the main parish in Registro, became the Economo (head of finances) for the Province of Sao

Paulo. He now lives in an SVD home for retired priests in Santo Amara, which he was instrumental in financing and building. I stayed in Registro for several years and I suppose this is where my interest in the medicinal properties of plants began.

CHAPTER 5

Bananas, Tea and Man's Inhumanity to Man

Bananas grew for kilometre stretches along the coast of Registro. Huge flourishes of them, plantations of them, and many of the indigenous population earned their living working in these plantations, some of them suffering the severe consequences of powerful insecticides. As a school pupil in Dublin, I had been taught that bananas were grown in Southeast Asia and had been introduced to Europe in the 17th century. In my mind they were always a luxurious reminder of the tropics, of exotic locations where sweet fruit was ready to be plucked all year round. I had never before associated bananas with Brazil, however it was here that I learned of their medicinal properties: their flesh for treating lung problems and the skin as a cure for scarring.

Another very important crop in Registro was tea. It is known as Chá in Brazil, and drunk mainly when sick, as again it is assumed to have medicinal purposes. The teas grown in Brazil have come from Japan, and this was another unexpected association for me – the Japanese in Brazil. Brazil is the home to the highest population of Japanese outside Japan. Immigration began in the early 1900s when the Italians that had come to work in the coffee plantations were repatriated. At this time there was a great deal of hunger in northern Japan and Brazil agreed for mass migration to begin, providing that they worked in the coffee plantations replacing the African slaves of the 19th century. The Japanese not only worked in horrendous conditions with very low pay, but they brought with them and cultivated the best Camellia Sinensis tea. This was made into black, green or white tea and thus the Chá Riviera was born.

For decades it provided employment for many of the indigenous people. However in the 80s and 90s the government imported cheaper teas, resulting in these plantations becoming abandoned but recently tea production has recommenced, with new organic methods, and the pride of the Valley of Ribeira is back in production.

As an avid tea drinker myself, both in Ireland and Brazil, I am lucky enough never to have contracted the deadly Amoemba infection – which can be rife in Brazil causing chronic dysentery and fever. I put this down to my copious black tea drinking – always with boiled water. As for its medicinal properties, Camellia Sinensis is best known for its ability to thin and purify the blood, it is an astringent, an analgesic, anti-asthmatic; antibacterial, antioxidant, digestive, diuretic, anti-diarrhoea; eliminates fats, helps weight reduction, lowers cholesterol and minimizes flu symptoms. I now realise why in Ireland tea is so popular with all these properties, and it was highly prized by the Japanese. I also learned that the leaves from the tea plant, had three different functions.

- White tea with antioxidant properties is obtained from the top of the plant and the very new leaves and the buds.
- Green tea is made with slightly older leaves that are passed through a steam chamber before being dried. Again, these are excellent antioxidants and have dietary properties.
- Black tea is made from the older leaves at the bottom of the plant. These can be crushed and fermented before drying. This is the cheapest type of tea, the least desirable going into tea bags.

The temperature of water is also crucial when preparing a tea: black can take temps up 97 degrees; green and white: 77 degrees – this is similar for other herbal treatments – with young leaves it is important not to damage them with boiling water – so a lower temperature is required.

So although there is nothing I like more than to sit back and enjoy a relaxing cup of tea, the reality is that I found so early in Brazil was the evidence of man's inhumanity to man. After all it was the slave trade that helped bring the banana to Europe. The British Empire, where it was once said that 'the sun never sets' due to its vastness, was at its colonial height between the 18th and 20th century. The British slave trade began in 1562, during the reign of Elizabeth I, when John Hawkins sold a group of Africans to the Spaniards of Santo Domingo in exchange for gold, sugar and leather. The Spaniards had most likely plundered South America for these goods, but within a short time the British dominated the slave trade in the Caribbean and the thirteen North American Colonies. In 1807 when slave trafficking was abolished in Britain, Brazil continued to engage the labour of transported slaves from Africa to work in their coffee and banana plantations until 1888 when it was abolished. By this time, an estimated 5.8 million Africans had been transported to Brazil. The figures are staggering and the evidence of enslavement and exploitation by the more powerful rulers, whether it be of the indigenous people, Africans, Italians (who were brought over as cheap labour to replace the Africans), and subsequently the Japanese, is all around you in Registro. There's no escaping it.

It reminds me in many ways of how the Great Famine of 1845-1851 resonates to this day with the Irish people. The evidence of the mass starvation when more than 1 million people were killed and another 1 million were forced to emigrate reducing the population by 25% still shocks. Indeed, in many eyes, it was unforgivable of the then British Government who did nothing to prevent it or send humanitarian aid. Charles Trevelyan, Her Majesty's Assistant Treasury Secretary in 1847 said:

"Hunger is God's punishment for an idle, ungrateful and rebellious country, and indolent and little self-sufficient people. The Irish suffer from an affliction of God's providence." He incidentally was made a Lord in 1848 for overseeing the hunger relief. James Connolly, co-leader of the Easter Rising in 1916 said,

"Providence sent the potato plague, but England made the hunger." The potato famine, caused by a disease that contaminated the whole of Ireland's potato crop, still grates in the psyche of Irish people today.

You can see now how my mind works! From plantations of bananas, tea and the Great Potato Famine in Ireland, and at the heart of it all, exploitation of workers, and man's inhumanity to man.

By 1978, after five years in Brazil, four of them in Registro, it was time for me to leave. The Bishop wanted me to stay and take over a parish in Eldorado. But I had already made my decision to leave. I had made great friends with everyone, but it was time for me to go.

CHAPTER 6

The Call of the Mountains

It was the mountains that led me to my life as a missionary and it was to the mountains I returned in 1978 on my first visit back to Europe. On my way to Ireland I had stopped off at Wetzlar near Frankfurt in Germany where I caught up with Annelise and Dom Hoeller, and from there I visited Sister Beth's family in Innsbruck. Her home was in the part of Austria that is surrounded by mountains in the Karwendel region. The first mountain I climbed was Lamsenspitz at 2508 metres and it felt amazing. Some missionaries, like Jose Freinadametz (one of the SVD's co-founders), never returned to their homeland. I rejoiced in the fact that I had completed five years in Brazil and had made it back to Europe.

I visited Sister Edel in Laupheim where I had worked when training as a missionary in 1970. It was so good to renew our friendship and to know that she, on the other side of the world, had been praying for me in the missions. And finally, I got back to Ireland to an amazing and emotional homecoming. 'The great missionary returns!! Hurrah!' At that time, my family consisted of my brothers, John and Vincent, my sisters, Julie and Mary and their husbands/wives and families, and most important of all, my mother, Mollie. What a celebration we had.

As a seminarian, I had studied at Maynooth in county Kildare where I had met Sister Meabh and Sister Irene, who were both now psychologists working with people with significant mental health problems. They had often come to my family home in Clontarf in Dublin and drunk tea with myself and my mother. It was lovely to see them again and we arranged to walk the Dublin Wicklow mountains and also the mountains of Mourne in Northern Ireland. I think the mountains of Mourne were a step too far for them, (22 miles - 34km) but for me it was wonderfully refreshing and invigorating.

During this summer back home in 1978, a significant event happened in Rome. Pope Paul VI passed away and a new Pope was elected. It took the cardinals 20 days to elect the new Pope John Paul I. Sadly, after only 33 days, he was found dead. He became known as the 'Pope of the Smile' because he was so affable. However, many people said he was murdered because of his progressive ideas. Maybe it was because he said we should see God as much more of a Mother than a Father figure? Whatever, it was a great shock and very unsettling to all of us working in the church at this time. In less than three weeks, another new pope was elected, Pope John Paul II and he held the post for 26 years and 5 months until his death in 2005. 1978 was forever to me the year of the three popes, and as I headed back to Brazil, (and to a new post), I vowed the next time I was back in Europe, I would visit the Vatican and Rome.

My new post was at St Marcos in the east side of Sao Paulo. And of course, the first thing I noticed when I arrived was the nearest mountain or perhaps hill (it wasn't quite a mountain!) And when I see a mountain, I need to climb it! I was told by the parishioners that it was called Morro Pelado – the bare hill and I felt it needed a better identity. St Marcos was in a densely populated area of Sao Paulo and in order to find the route up the hill, I had to pass through the neighbourhoods of Rodolfo Pirani and Jardim Santo André. I eventually found a trail that would take me up the hill. As I reached the summit and saw the neighbourhoods below, I thought what a beautiful place it would be to put up a cross.

So with the parishioners, a few planks of wood and some concrete, we planned the walk. It was a great procession as we made our way up the trail with young and elderly alike. We prayed at the top, thanking God for the vista and our health and our cross was finally erected. From now on, the hill would be known as the Morro do Cruzeiro (Hill of the Cross). But unfortunately it didn't last long. It was soon vandalised and the wood trashed and thrown down the hill. We made three more crosses, each one stronger than the other, but the religious intolerance surrounding the area was stronger than I had ever anticipated, and each time we replaced the cross, it was ceremoniously broken and thrown down the hill. Nonetheless, each time, it was always a great pleasure to climb that hill and now bizarrely it is known as Morro do Sabao – Soap Hill for whatever reason, I have no idea.

The parish of St Marcos was located in a very poor area and the buildings were fairly basic. Many of the streets, including that of the parish were not yet laid. Cement paving blocks were lined up outside, but it took a long time for the asphalt and the roads to be laid. Inside the parish house, I felt immediately at home and Father Pedro Barendse was instrumental in introducing me to the new parish community. His approach was to persuade people through Catechesis, ie: religious instruction through the sacraments. I had worked in Registro and had led groups through gospel readings in communities but Father Pedro's approach was different and his aim was for every parish to take the form of a Christian community through the sacraments. It was a very successful approach and this is how he did it.

He established 'Friendship Groups' for parents whose children would be making their First Communion in the coming year. After

Sunday Mass, he organised the children to go to catechists, and the parents to meet in their friendship groups where they would hear about the teachings linked to their child's class. Many parents knew little about their faith, but this friendship group enabled them to participate in the learning process and they were given follow up activities to continue the learning with the children during the week. The parents in these groups became true friends, and true Christian leaders, many of whom volunteered to become catechists in the future.

Another area I began working in was in pastoral health. Father David Vantrob was an SVD priest working as a Chaplain in the Municipal Hospital of Tatuapé. He needed some help and I was asked to go there on Monday mornings to assist him. One of the priests at St Marcos loaned me his motorbike to get there and I remember that Monday mornings in the accident and emergency rooms were pandemonium. On my first day I found a man lying on stretcher bed shouting continuously,

"Doctor! Doctor! I want a doctor." And I went over to him and quietly said,

"Can I help you?" and he asked me if I was a doctor, and I said no, that I was a priest. He took one look at me, and shouted,

"A priest! A priest! I don't want to die!!!" and he jumped off the stretcher trolley and ran out of the hospital never to be seen again. I was so embarrassed. But Father Vantrob reassured me and encouraged me to come back every Monday morning to help pacify the patients.

There were 9 floors in the hospital and I realised there was lots to be done. I worked with volunteers and we shared the workload between us. I was very sorry to leave after 6 months when the bishop asked me to stand down to allow another priest in need of a job to take over. However there was a great deal of health work to do back in the parish and I was able to continue visiting the hospital in the afternoons and evenings.

Around the same time, in 1981 there was a new Pastoral Health Movement in the church that proposed three dimensions to make it more holistic and to influence the nation's health policy. These dimensions were:

- **Solidarity**: Samaritan experience and presence with the sick and suffering in health institutions, in families and in the community. It aimed to serve the individual fully in the physical, psychological, social and spiritual dimension.
- **Community**: Health promotion and education. It related to public health, acting on disease

prevention. It sought to value wisdom and popular religious customs in relation to health.

- **Political-Institutional**: Public and private institutions that trained health professionals and provided services in the health sector. It ensured bioethical reflection, ethical training and a health policy in order that agents were articulators and supervisors of decisions in health and actively participating in the Health Councils.

Having worked in hospitals in England, Ireland and Germany, and my recent time spent in the hospital at Tatuapé, I felt I had enough experience to set to work in two of these dimensions in the parish: Solidarity and Community. I trained a group of voluntary lay people and discussed with them on how to visit the sick, what to say, what not to say, and how to leave the patient with an uplifting feeling. We visited at all times of the day within the parish week. And after a while we received an invitation to go to the nearby parish of St Mateus for a lecture on health. The lecturers were Dr José Augusto and Dr Eduardo Jorge, both general practitioners from north-eastern Brazil. We had assumed the lecture would be a continuation of our pastoral work, but this meeting was inspirational and ground-breaking. They spoke of the need to have clinics and health centres to serve the poorest in the neighbourhood.

They needed the people to become organised and articulate to make the health authorities aware of their needs in this poverty-stricken area of the east side of Sao Paulo.

From this meeting we were motivated to organise an election for two community leaders to represent the people for our own health council. Voting was done over two weekends, and we printed out photos and background information on the candidates. Sealed ballot boxes were made and volunteers ensured voting was done privately. The same committed volunteers of the Nossa Senhora das Graças community counted the votes and declared the winners. The elected candidates were presented to the Health Council, and the director of public health for Sao Paulo, Dr Adib Jatene, a cardiologist was invited to St Mateus parish to meet the health representatives. He listened sensitively to their concerns and he looked at the courtyard behind the church where the community believed a health centre should be located. Their request was a success, and soon a survey of the land was undertaken and not only was a Health Centre built, but a hospital too. This is known today as the Hospital of Nossa Senhora das Graças and has served the people of south-eastern Sao Paulo to this day.

I was so happy with this transformational approach of faith into action and I wanted to continue to empower the locals to improve their quality of life. Already I had had success with the leadership groups in Registro; the friendship groups in St Marcos and now the creation of a Health Clinic and Hospital for the parish of St Mateus. I was a true Liberation Theologist.

CHAPTER 7

Gone Too Soon

As a missionary priest you help to mark the most significant occasions in life: births, deaths and marriages, (not unlike a local newspaper.) And of course, as a priest you add to each life a sense of dignity, purpose, and uniqueness. Each life, no matter how challenged or lowly, is important in God's plan. And no one had a greater plan or purpose on earth I'm sure than Sister Ofélia. I first met her in the parish of St Mateus where she worked in the daycare centre. She was so popular with the local people that they even named the creche after her. There was nothing she wouldn't do for the children or their parents. However, one day she came to speak with me in a confused state. She was pregnant, and the father of her baby was a local priest whom she had had a brief relationship with. I said I'd come with her to speak with our Bishop, Dom Luciano, who would need to know why she would be giving up her work at the creche.

In tears she told Dom Luciano that she was expecting a child, and in reply the 'sainted' Luciano said:

"How wonderful! What a blessing!"

Sister Ofélia's wounded soul was immediately healed and she cried and cried and so did I. Luciano organised a place for her to go in Lumiar, not far from Nova Friburgo and he asked if I could continue to be involved in the welfare of mother and baby. I agreed, and when I went to visit her each month, the Bishop in the community assumed that I was the father! Once I explained the situation, the Bishop would come and visit her too. Over the coming months I provided support and friendship until Julius Rodriguez was born on the 8th July 1979 and I felt so privileged to have done this. Dom Luciano baptised Julius at a convent of the Sisters of the Holy Spirit in Tatuapé. Ofelia returned to her own name of Maria Joana and continued her studies for a degree in Social Work. Sister Eloine was like a mother to her and after graduating Ofélia went to work with abandoned babies, many of whom were born with AIDS in the Sao Paulo organisation of the Foundation for Child Welfare. (FEBEM) Princess Diana visited FEBEM in 1991 where she was extensively photographed with the children playing with a gold cross and chain she was wearing.

When Ofélia retired, she went back to her hometown of Marilia to work with plants and herbs, and sadly, in 2013, on the farm which she had bought, she fell into the pond and tragically drowned. Ofelia's son Julius went on to become a lawyer and married a girl who is an Evangelist like himself. We still keep in touch. He calls me Uncle Joe!

Antonio Meroth was a young priest who I worked with in a team at St Marcos that included Nicolau Bakker and Sister Angela. We were a close-knit 'team' at the parish, especially when Father Pedro Barendse left to work in another mission and we had responsibility for building communities and spreading the word. In 1983, while I was in Rome, I heard the news that Antonio had been killed in a freak motorcycle accident. I didn't know until then how much he had influenced my life. Here is an extract from the memoir of Antonio Meroth, that was written in 2020 by Fernando Altemeyer Junior:

4th March 1983: *Father Antonio Meroth, a Catholic priest of German nationality, born in Christanzhofen, in 1948, ordained a priest in the city of Rottemburg, Germany, in 1976. Member of the Society of the Divine Word - or more simply SVD. Sent to Brazil, he worked for some time at Água Rasa with the youth and was soon sent to the St Marcos Church, in Parque St Rafael, on the outskirts of the East Zone of São Paulo.*

He was deeply involved in the social and organizational life of his neighbourhood, the ABC dormitory area., marked by a strong steelwork presence and social struggles. He died due to lack of adequate help from a motorcycle accident that occurred at Rua Domiziano Rossi, in São Mateus.

He died as a poor man without an ambulance to take him to the hospital that was prepared to act on his case, which was very serious. The private clinic on Avenida Mateo Bei refused to accept the cheque from the police officer who helped him, because they wanted the 2,000 Reais for the ambulance in cash only. So when they heard that he was a priest and Father Nicolau came to help him, but by then it was too late.

There was a memorial mass for Antonio in the middle of the Avenue, that brought the traffic to a halt of the entire East Zone. Here was Antonio, fighting for injustice, and dying of an injustice that he did not have enough ready cash to pay for his hospital treatment.

I was in staying in Nemi, a village south of Rome, when I heard about Antonio's death. I was so upset. I had gone on vacation to celebrate my ten years as a priest, and I had set out my goals as: to climb the Mattehorn in Switzerland; to reflect on my next direction; and to bring my mother to Rome. I never imagined that I would be grieving a fellow priest, who was only 37 years old, and who had done so much on bringing faiths together in ecumenism. Along with Antonio, I also heard that Sister Angela, who had worked with us in St Marcos, had also been killed in a freak accident while travelling. A bus-tyre had exploded, and the wheel rim came flying off and struck Sister Angela killing her instantly. I went out walking as soon as I'd heard of their deaths. I walked up Monte Lupone and in those days there were no mobile phones or Facebook messages to share details. I felt very much alone, but somehow, very much with Antonio and Sister Angela. As I celebrated mass in their memory on the mountain, the tears I shed flowed into the chalice that I consecrated and shared their passion with Christ. I left a cross in the space where I celebrated this holy place.

Back at the Divine Word Centre in Nemi, Sister Therese, a psychotherapist, was waiting for me and wanted to know where I'd been as I came back so late. I knew that the path I needed direction in was psychological, to understand the emotional aspect of life as well as the spiritual. I had been looking for direction in this area and had semi-agreed to be guided by a priest. However, after undertaking the Myles Briggs Personality Type assessment and talking about my emotional experience on Monte Lupone, Sister Therese agreed to be my spiritual director during my stay in Nemi, and she wanted to see the holy place on Monte Lupone. Along with some visiting sisters from Australia and New Zealand, we had a wonderful experience climbing Monte Lupone, and I was so glad the sisters had a van waiting at the base of the mountain to take them back to the centre, as it had been an arduous climb. I felt then that the burden of grief and sadness of the deaths of my friends and fellow team members, Antonio and Sister Angela, had been lifted

My mother arrived in Rome and we had a great celebration at the SVD Centre in Nemi. She bought cakes for everyone and decorated them for the teachers and leaders in the centre. Sometimes she'd decorate them with a biblical quotation, – some of these I would have quoted in my letters when I couldn't think of anything else to say. She thought I was so learned and scholarly after my ten years as a priest. I was delighted to introduce her to 'Mother Theresa', my spiritual directress, and my mother remarked that she was so gentle, she'd be too 'soft' to direct me! But she adored Sister Theresa all the same. My mother saw beauty in everything. She arrived full of faith and left with it still intact!! I took her everywhere and she felt honoured and treated like a 'queen' wherever she went. It was only as I said goodbye to her at Rome airport that I realised what age she was when I held her passport. She was 80 years old. She died six years later in 1989, aged 86 years. She, like Sister Ofélia, Father Antonio and Sister Angela, left a lasting impression on me, and were gone too soon

CHAPTER 8

So Long, Farewell

It's impossible to visit St Peter's Basilica in Rome and not be impressed by the works of art. Michelangelo's La Pieta was such a moving and magnificent sculpture. I couldn't understand how someone so young could accomplish something so perfect. I also saw a very beautiful painting of Our Lady pregnant (Madonna del Parto) which I learned was an iconic style of painting developed in 14th century Italy. St Peter's Basilica in Rome was remarkable, but I think I prefer a smaller church for prayer. Outside in St Peter's Square, I met Pope John Paul II.

"Hi, I'm from Brazil," I said, and he replied in Portuguese: "So God Bless you."

The group of priests I was studying with at the SVD centre in Nemi were Donal Daly, a professor from Maynooth University, who had been my Philosophy tutor at the seminary in Roscommon; Tony Doyle and Noel Carrol who were both English missionaries in Ecuador. We attended John Fuellenbach's lectures on Liberation Theology in Latin America and I felt at home as he talked about the work of the Basic Christian Communities (CEBs) and the way things should be done.

A trip to Florence was arranged for our group and as I had kept in touch with a nurse I had worked with in the hospital of St Olave's in London, and I discovered that by coincidence, she was in Italy at the same time, caring for a patient in the Tuscany region. While the other priests visited works of art, I arranged to meet Joanne. I was so worried that we wouldn't recognise each other. It was 14 years since I'd worked with her and even although we'd both changed, we couldn't miss each other outside Our Lady of Flowers (Igreja Matiz) church in Florence. Later, I invited Joanne to return with us to the SVD centre in Nemi and she was made so welcome by everyone, and she had a wonderful time. Joanne remained a good friend of mine. She supported me after my mother passed away in 1989, when I visited her in London, and she came to my 25th anniversary celebrations in Dublin in 1998.

In Europe that year, my goal had always been to climb the Mattehorne, but I had an accident and damaged my ribs, so it wasn't to be. Instead I climbed some lesser mountains in Innsbruck in Austria with Sister Beth's nephews and I did lots of walking. My next stop was to visit Antonio Meroth's sister in Germany. I had planned to do a slide show there, to show her some of his work, but unfortunately I had left the slides behind in Austria. However, just as it dawned on me that my slides were missing, Sister Beth's nephews arrived in Germany with them, and they were able to translate my whole commentary as my German isn't great. Divine Intervention or what!!!? My next step before heading to Ireland was to visit Sister Edel in Laupheim. And I couldn't leave Germany without a visit to my missionary Godparents: Frau Annelise and Herr Hoeller – where we chatted and I picked the most delicious cherries from their back garden. At that moment in time I once again thought: what a hard life it is to be a missionary!

After fond farewells it was time to visit my family in Clontarf in Dublin, to return to my family home we called number 39. It had been the centre of our universe growing up. We had spent many happy times together. My father passed away in 1966, I entered the seminary in 1967, and my mother lived at number 39 for another 22 years. There were numerous family celebrations for my return and many sad farewells as I departed.

Italy, Austria, Germany and Ireland, it was time for me to go back to Brazil and when I returned to St Marcos, I knew it would only be for a short time, as I was being sent, or rather I had chosen to go to Santarém, deep in the Amazon Basin. The Divine Word Mission in Sao Paulo had no missionaries in this region of Brazil. Up until then it had been the Franciscans who worked in this area, but they were finding life there difficult. It was both a challenge and an honour for me to be the first SVD missionary to work in this area. There were so many farewells from the communities I had worked in and from all the priests I had worked with in my ten years in Sao Paulo. I was serenaded all the way to the airport and even Nina, whom I had known as Cida in Registro, and who was now living in the St Marcos community, came to say farewell. It didn't seem long since I'd said goodbye to her in Registro and I was sure that we would meet again.

The small city of Santarém was a six-hour flight away from Sao Paulo and lies on the banks of the Amazon in the state of Para. It is in a lake area where the River Tapajos meets the River Amazon and both rivers converge and then flow side by side for kilometres. It was once home to the indigenous Tapajos people who managed a large, prosperous agricultural chiefdom, before the Portuguese came and took it over in the 1600s.

I had expected my new role to be a riverboat priest, visiting communities by river as there were no roads or tracks to travel by land. However, when I arrived at the assigned church, the parish priest, who was Italian, Fr Atilio, was barely coping. His father was dying and he was desperate to get back to Italy to see him. Within a week of my arrival, after giving me a quick tour of the church, the parish house and the community, he said farewell and never returned. Therefore, instead of taking up my missionary post as a boat priest, I found myself responsible for two parishes: St Raimundo Nonato and Fatima. A family from the distant area of Arapixuna had been appointed by Fr Atilio to take care of the house, sacristy, and administration, but they too said farewell to me within a year. And here I found myself alone, with two parishes and in addition, the river communities of Arapuins, Arua and Maro to serve. Thank goodness for the Franciscan priests and sisters, some of whom worked in the local hospital, for inviting me to socialise at Sunday evening dinners. They were lifesavers, even although some of them were weary and wanted to leave too like Fr Atilio.

I didn't realise then that it would a riverboat that would save me and prevent me from saying farewell to Santarém too. It wasn't just the boat, but also a young German named Rainer from Wetzlar, who was travelling in Brazil researching the work of missionaries. The day he walked into St Raimundo's church, my prayers were answered. The Francisicans had a boat called the San Francisco that had served the communities of the Arapiuns River for many years. Bishop Dom Tiago Ryan asked if I would accompany them in their work and I was joined by two other missionaries. As my work with the communities developed in the region of Arapixuna, and the other missionaries were posted elsewhere, I realised that I needed a boat of my own: - an SVD boat, but unfortunately the SVD in Sao Paulo were unable to fund the significant sum required.

Just at this time, Rainer Neubar arrived in my parish of St Raimundo's looking for a priest who would take him to visit the communities upriver. He was with his girlfriend and they were learning about the Brazilian way of life. He later wrote to me saying:

"I found you entering the St Raimundo Church in Santarém in 1984. At that time I was travelling through Brazil for six months, visiting several missionaries to learn about their work and about the lives of the people in Brazil. I just arrived from Obidos where I had spent a few days with Franciscan priests, who were very disillusioned by the 'work' being done by 'missionaries'. The Franciscans of Obidos sent me to those in Santarém (Americans) who sent me to St Raimundo.

I entered the church and at that moment another world was opened to me. Here was a priest who was not there at the altar, talking over people's heads, but here was a priest who was walking amongst the people, talking to people, speaking in the language of the people, telling jokes and stories that had something to do with the lives of each one present. Here was a living priest in contato with the community and everyone was looking at him, following his words, fascinated by the energy of this extraordinary priest. It was the first moment on my trip through Brazil when I felt that there truly is this living church that I was looking for. After mass I talked to you about what I was looking for, and I soon found myself on your boat with some seminarians and making my first visit to Cuipuiranga...."

Using the San Francisco boat, I asked Rainer and his girlfriend to join us. We were working on a project to help the river communities catch more fish and we were engaged in cutting a trail through the thick vegetation that would allow a route through from the River Arapiuns to the River Amazon for the fishermen to access more fish. They had been limited by their catches by random 'bombers' placing explosives in the river to kill the fish, which seemed to them a quicker method of fishing than using nets or having to cut through the vegetation. Unfortunately, they were killing shoals of fish and destroying the habitat for years to come. So armed with machetes and large knives, we cut a route through, singing hymns as we went. We reached a clearing and had a celebration for the successful completion of the fishing route.

Rainer and his girlfriend took photos, and I asked him to get in touch with my Godparents in Wetzlar when he got back to Germany, Frau Annelise and Herr Hoeller who I had only so recently eaten cherries in their back garden. Frau Hoeller sent the photos of us clearing the vegetation in the Amazon to Father

Manfred Link in Germany who had recently returned from missionary work in Bahia in Brazil. On seeing the photos and listening to Rainer's story, he agreed that this was missionary work he could fund. With the support of Rainer and Father Manfred in Wetzlar, my pastoral work is still being funded today.

When Rainer returned to Santarém, this time with a new girlfriend, who would later become his wife, and with the desire to base his academic thesis on the work of the river people, I was pleased to welcome him aboard my new riverboat: the Antonio Meroth, and the people called it Meroti for short. Rainer continued to work with me and the youth of the river for the next few years.

CHAPTER 9

Tales from the Riverboat

We had many memorable incidents on the river boat and with the communities we worked in. Once after a full week's work up river we were heading back to Santarém at night. Typically the boat was full of hitchhikers all looking for a free trip into the city. Pedrau, one of the villagers from Piaui, said he'd be the pilot for the trip and I agreed, but halfway through the sail, Rainer came to me in a panic saying that Pedrau had fallen asleep and a huge ferry ship carrying quarry stones was heading straight for us. When I got to the helm I realised that our night lights weren't on! Rainer grabbed the wheel while I put on the searchlights and mandatory lamps. We veered out of the way just in time, but we were close enough to hear the swearing and shouting of the crew of the ferry over the throb of our boat engine. It was a close shave, and as you can imagine, we were all so relieved that we sang Glorias and thanksgivings all the way back to Santarém.

It was usual to be away on the riverboat for a week or more at a time, visiting the communities. The staple diet was beiju flour and fish. Beiju flour is a starchy tapioca made from the cassava root, and once ground, dried and then mixed with water, it is heated as a flatbread and eaten with fish. It has been a known staple in the northern area of Brazil since the Portuguese first recorded it in 1618. After a week of beiju and fish followed by fish and beiju, I yearned for the taste of real bread, and any ingredient other than fish. When I took the boat back to the parish in Santarém, I usually docked in the quay outside St Raimundo's Convent. The sisters told me that when the chickens in the yard heard the boat engine approaching, they fled into the bush, for fear of being sent to their graveyard, in the priest's belly! I always tried to be back at St Raimundo's by 4 o'clock in afternoon. This allowed me to shower and change before the *carapanas* (mosquitoes) came out. I would hold a penitential service before hearing confessions, and then I'd retire to the boat where I slept. I would close the windows tight, as I figured it was easier to sweat a little in the night than be devoured by the *carapanas*. The next day, I would say mass at 9am and the people would come from every corner, some by boat, some from the bush, and some having walked for miles.

There was always something to fix on the boat; if it wasn't the radio or the record player, it was the 25-horsepower engine. Luiz, a member of the community came to help me and soon learned how to pilot the boat. Sister Manoelina travelled in the boat, speaking to the women in the river communities about health and welfare.

Keeping healthy and clean in this part of the world is difficult especially when there is so little fresh water. In one community on the Amazon River, we managed to drill a well and when we saw the water gushing out, the women burst into tears of joy. Previously they would have had to descend 200 metres and then ascend the hill carrying 18 litres of water on their heads, several times a day. This engineering feat by Frei Mauro, a Fransciscan, and his team, was life changing. Unfortunately we weren't able to do this in every community, but at least in Aninduba, which was the highest community in the Amazon, we were successful.

Another community I worked in was called Laranjal. I usually arrived in the afternoon and would meet with the leaders to prepare for penitential services and confession later. I was expected to sleep in a hammock in the sacristy but on one occasion, after the service was over, a bat passed over me with a rush. The wind from its flight gave off the distinct odour that these bats have. I used a broom and managed to kill it. (I ask forgiveness of bat lovers.) I'd never seen such an ugly creature in my life - the fangs it had for teeth! As well as bats, the sacristy was full of carapanas, so I decided that it was safer to sleep on the boat. As it was dark, I used my torch to guide my path. Once on board, I slept in my hammock but I was awakened by a noise on the boat's awning. I turned on the torch to have a look outside but I could see nothing. After a while, I decided it must have been a branch of a tree that had fallen and went back to my hammock, but I didn't sleep much. The next morning I left early to say mass in the community. I mentioned the crashing noise that had disturbed my sleep, but no one could suggest what it may have been. After mass I went to visit another community on the Amazon called Vila Guajara where I had arranged to meet with a youth group. On my way back to the boat I was determined to find out what had crashed onto my awning the night before, so I prodded under a box until I discovered a huge mother rat with a dozen babies! I showed no mercy – and sent them all fleeing into the Amazon River. It had been a close encounter.

There were times on the Meroti that I felt like a pirate with the knife between my teeth, as I clambered down the stern steps to clear the long grasses entangled in the boat propellors. In the murky brown waters, at night I would see alligators' eyes illuminated by the spotlights, but I never felt afraid of these. I was more wary of the nests of ants that floated down river in the grasses. Some of these nests had snakes hidden in them and would strike if you tried to fight them off. Luckily I never came across a snake. The jararaca is the deadliest snake in this area, the word means 'large snake' and it is a venomous viper with a deadly snakebite. All along the river, the people built their houses on stilts and when the waters rose, they would need to move inland where it was drier. Those that stayed found it difficult to live in the turbulent waters. One such person was Rosivete, a teacher and a community coordinator. She visited her pupils on her canoe each day, paddling bravely against the currents. When I said mass in the communities, some families would gift me manioc flour made from the cassava root, and a live chicken. I would bring these to Rosivete and she would make delicious chicken soup and bread as a treat for her father and me.

Rainer, along with nuns from the local hospital, were part of the team that delivered courses to the communities promoting healthy eating using nutritious fruit and vegetables and fighting common diseases with hygienic practices. We were always made welcome and at the end of each course, we'd celebrate with a mass of thanksgiving. Along with the practical, I always had at the back of my mind, the need to find ways of communicating Christ's message in a relevant and enjoyable way. Father Jose de Anchieta was a Spanish missionary who worked in Brazil from 1534 to 1597 and he was also a poet and a playwright. He was canonized by Pope Francis in 2014, but back in the 1980s when I worked upriver, he was my inspiration. He believed in using literature and theatre and he even learned the indigenous language of Tupi to share the evangelical message of Christ. At night, on the riverboat, I never felt alone without television and with only an oil lamp for light, I began to write my plays, based on the gospels of Christ.

CHAPTER 10

The Show Must Go On

Following in Fr Jose de Anchieta's footsteps, we formed a theatre group and our first play was performed on Good Friday in 1984. It was so successful that we re-enacted it each year until 1988. We based it on the Gospels of St John and translated some of the lyrics from the play: 'Jesus Christ Superstar'. The scene in the Garden of Gethsemane always created an intense atmosphere especially in 1988 which was the year of the Brazilian Campaign of Fraternity and marked 100 years of the abolition of slavery in 1888. In Jesus' suffering in Gethsemane when he was betrayed, 'I heard the cry of this people,' and I vividly remember the moving emotion of that scene as it was performed in Santarém. We took our production to the communities of Cuipiranga and Arapiuns. We connected the light and power from a boat and we set up the stage and equipment on the beach. The audience sat on the sand. It was wonderful.

Each actor who played Jesus had the freedom to improvise from their reading and understanding of the scriptures. The actor from the Workers' Party played Jesus as someone who defended the poor workers. The Catholic Charismatic actors would present a more moderate and spiritual Jesus.

Another play we produced was Meratnas, (Santarém in reverse), and it was about the history of Brazil from Noah's Ark. It was a teenage youth group and everyone wanted a part in this play. We also took the Easter play to Sao Sebastien, an area of the city that had better facilities with a real stage and dressing rooms. Now nobody said not to have a drink during the performance, and on this occasion, when the servant asked Peter

"Were you not with him?" Peter did not deny it, but drunkenly replied. "Do you not know who you're talking to? I am St Peter, a great friend of Jesus," At this point, I needed to cut the microphones and sound system so that no more nonsense could be heard. And in this same performance, the cockerel recording didn't work, and someone improvised, and it sounded like the chicken had been strangled. But that's theatre – and as we all know, the show must go on. Already the seeds had begun to bear fruit, as several of the actors married and their offspring currently participate in the life of the theatre as their parents did then.

Anyone who has ever produced a play will know how exhausting it is. The rehearsals, the directions, organising costumes, sets, lighting and an audience. It takes a huge amount of energy and commitment.

Reproducing scripts was especially difficult, as there was no easy access to a photocopier. But the rewards were bountiful. Each missionary needs to find their own way of sharing the Word with their people. Now in the digital days of WhatsApp and Facebook, new ways will be tried and tested, but back in the 1980s, I found that by following in the footsteps of the great St Jose de Anchieta, and putting on performances, I achieved so much.

CHAPTER 11

Shipwreck

It wasn't the shipwreck that was the final straw, it wasn't the mosquitoes that somehow wanted to take part in my sermons, and it wasn't the theatre groups that did it, but I was having some health issues, kidney stones, and the pain had become so unbearable I needed an operation. I was also having trouble with a deviated septum in my nose, and maybe it wasn't wise to undergo two operations in the same year, but I felt it was necessary. Unfortunately it was not practical for me to convalesce in Sao Paulo or Santarém, so I decided to take a vacation and go back to Ireland. However, I was no sooner back when I suffered an even more traumatic injury when I visited a church and a swinging door slammed into my face causing my nose to bleed profusely. My family were waiting to celebrate my homecoming, but instead I was taken to hospital and lost so much blood I was unable to be a blood donor for a long time to come. This upset me more than anything, as I was always a regular blood donor.

That summer in Ireland I had plenty of time to reflect on my life in the Amazon: the porters at the piers in Santarém when the tide was out, walking for miles carrying sacks and sacks of flour on their backs, pushing their necks forward and ruining their posture for life; the ever present mosquitoes in the heat: the last mass I had given in Vila Franca the mosquitoes were so bad, they got under my vestments and I had to throw myself into the river when I got back to my boat in order to kill them off. I wasn't taking them onto the boat with me. I smiled to myself too as I thought of the chaotic church processions carrying images of the saints and Our Lady on long poles out into the communities. Once when we attached a loudspeaker onto a pole so that our hymns and prayers could be heard, an elderly man bowed to the loudspeaker as though it was a new religious icon.

My life as a priest was important to the river communities especially for their baptismal certificates. These were like gold dust and meant the parents wouldn't be fined for not registering their child. As there were no calendars, we'd choose a saint's day as near to the birth as possible and it meant each child was validated and their birth recorded. Another important highlight was when I was sent as a representative to a conference in Curitiba in the southern province of Brazil as the only SVD priest working in the Amazon. I had so much information to share, of what improvements were needed to help transform lives, but no one asked me a single question. And of course, tugging at my heart strings were the theatre groups I'd started – the Easter plays were such a success and as I gathered my strength in Ireland, I knew then that I wasn't yet ready to leave Santarém and the river communities.

Before returning I went to visit my friends in Wetzlar in Germany. Fr Manfred was so welcoming and wrote an article for the local paper highlighting my work.

"Jose Dillon takes care of a parish in Santarem and 47 river community parishes. They live in difficult conditions and each parish has between 10 – 80 families with three to four generations living in each house. To work on the river, Jose must sleep 10 – 14 days on his boat. And he visits each community by bike inland on the jungle paths. To reach parishioners on the vast Amazon River, he pilots a small houseboat, and he takes care of weddings and baptisms and celebrates every feast day with all the communities. The economic situation is seriously compromised with the rise in commodity prices, the value of their own products is decreasing and their way of life is becoming harder. Jose Dillon speaks of his evangelical work with pride and passion."

I was so grateful for Fr Manfred's words. He became a great friend, and in later years, in another parish, he was responsible for my church in Sao Paulo having a sister church which we twinned with in Germany.

Back in Santarém there was still a lot to do with the theatre, the bible studies groups and the everyday work of the parish communities. Fr Waldir helped with the community work, and Fr Joao Mors took over the running of St Raimondo's which left me free to work in the river, but my health was still an issue. One day, while making our way to Urucurea, a terrible wind blew up, a real '*Venta Cima*'. We decided to tie the boat up in Vila Franca, at a sheltered beach. I placed the ropes on the starboard side, but overnight the wind direction changed and began beating the boat on the port side. The wind got stronger and I could not turn the stern, and the boat was thrown against the beach breaking the hull. That morning some other boats came to help push the boat off the beach, but she began to sink. Another boat came and managed to tow Meroti away to a shipyard. There was too much damage and it was too costly to repair. I realised then that my days as a riverboat priest were over.

That happened on November 2nd 1988, and within a couple of days I had a river christening to undertake on the River Tapajos. I couldn't let the parents of the baby down, so I managed to borrow a boat, but I knew then that I would soon return to Sao Paulo. I spoke with the Provincial, who told me that this would not be possible. But I had already been in touch with my good friend Mick MacGuiness who was now the Provincial of Sao Paulo and he said he would find a parish for me. I was determined to find a parish that was in the Aparecida area of Sao Paulo. And I also knew that I would be back to visit the Santarém people and the communities in another capacity in the future.

1.

2.

3.

4.

5.

6.

1.Karl, aged 98 in Germany, still with meaning and purpose to his life. 2. Joanne, a nurse and lifelong friend who I met when I worked as a student in London. 3. Sister Edel, from Laupheim in Germany who has prayed for me throughout my 50 years in Brazil. 4. Ellie Larkin (1st on left with the hat) at my first mass, in the Sacred Heart Home for the Elderly in Roscommon. 5.Annelise Hoeller, my Divine Word Missionary 'Godmother', who I stayed with in Germany before I left for Brazil in 1973. 6. My family in Dublin, (ltr) Mary, Vincen, Me, mum, John and Julie at my ordination.

7.

8.

9.

10.

11.

12.

7. Mercedes my first teacher of Portuguese. She corrected my grammar and encouraged my pronunciation. 8. The old VW van that we filled with youth leaders and dropped off at each community. 9. The shack that I started using as a chapel in 1978 in the parish of St Mark's. The people living in this shack later became caretakers in the main church. 10. The banana plantations on the coast of Registro. 11. The excavation begins for the construction of the John Paul II church in 1981. 12. One of the many chapels I said mass in on the banks of the River Amazon.

13.

14.

15.

16.

17.

18.

19.

13. Ofelia with her young son Julius 14. Antonio Meroth, the young priest I worked with in St Marcos 15. All along the river, the people built their houses on stilts. 16. When the rivers rose, they would need to move inland where it was drier. 17. Rainer the young student who visited Santarem and continued to work with me and the youth of the river for the next few years. 18. My riverboat, Antonio Meroth, that the people called 'Meroti'. 19. Increased rainfall due to climate change is causing great flooding in the communities due to rising levels of the rivers.

21.

20.

22.

23.

24.

20. The tinctures ready to be used. 22. Training therapists in the remote Rondonia state, north-west Brazil. 21. The health clinics in Sao Paulo where the remedies are distilled using the plant extracts. 23. Prayers of thanks for all that has been learned. 24. Time for some rest and reflection on my way back to Sao Paulo with some medicinal plants at my side.

CHAPTER 12

Where There is Despair

Returning to Sao Paulo, to the area of Jardim Miriam (Jardim means garden, but there was no such thing as a garden anywhere near this neighbourhood), in 1989, was like the lawless Wild West and one of the most crime ridden areas in Brazil. However, I was keen to get to know my parishioners, and to discover ways in which I could best serve them. The parish I was working in was Nossa Senhora Aparecida (Our Lady of Aparecida) which was in the middle of this unforgiving neighbourhood rife with gangs, guns, and drugs. Lucas Mouro, the international footballer, was raised in this area. It was when he witnessed a robbery at gunpoint at 8 years old while kicking a ball around in his street, that he decided that he wanted a better life for his family. This motivated him to work hard to get out of the area. For me, well it was dangerous, and I tried to keep an eye open for risks, but I realised that not all the people were gangsters and drug dealers. There were very good people living in this neighbourhood and if it weren't for them, it would have been difficult for me to work there. In order to develop myself, I took a course at the University in Ipiranga in bible studies, in particular the gospels of St John. And I undertook a course on Phytotherapy –

herbal medicines that are an effective and more affordable treatment to prescription drugs. These courses were to have a significant impact on my missionary work.

I remained in Jardin Miriam for more than 15 years as Parish Priest with responsibility for 7 other communities. There was so much work to do, but equally I had so much energy then. Much of my work was in prayer groups that took place in parishioners' homes in the evenings, but sometimes we had to cancel these abruptly because of gunfights between drug dealers outside in the streets. I lived at the back of a community in Jardim Luzo and directly beside my house was a favela and a stairway leading down to another world.......... really the end of the world. But it was here that I felt most useful. I set up a clinic at the back of our parish to discuss and administer treatments using herbal remedies. At the same time, a colleague I had worked with in Germany contacted me to say she and her husband were coming to Brazil. Her husband was the director of Bach's Flower Remedies, and she asked if I would be interested in hearing about these? It was such a coincidence, and with the knowledge I gained from Bach Remedies through courses run by Dr Lucia de Bartello, I was able to suggest our parish be a basis for training and work programmes. Accompanied by Dr Bartello's students and interns, and with my expertise in herbal remedies, our clinic began to expand slowly but surely, until there were queues at the door.

I was to become more and more involved in the emotional wellbeing of my parishioners and I had found my role. Surrounded by so much terror, death and violence in the outside environment, the flower and herbal remedies were a godsend. It gave the parishioners somewhere to breathe, to let go of their anxieties and worries, and to provide them with some hope that their situation would improve. At this time a new president, Fernando Collor de Mello came to power in Brazil and he immediately confiscated all the people's savings accounts. There was so much despair at this time, the clinic allowed people to vent their anger, and the herbal and flower remedies had a calming and restorative effect.

One of the communities I served was called St Antonio's. It had no church, in fact, the parishioners met in the house of a lady called Dona Antonia. Maria de Jesus oversaw this community, and with the funding from Wetzlar in Germany, we managed to buy a small house that would soon be demolished to begin the construction of a chapel. We contacted Luiza Erundina, the mayor of Sao Paulo and representative of the Workers' Party, (the best mayor I think there has ever been in Sao Paulo) She sent us twenty trucks to help excavate the site in preparation for the foundations. At first we planned to have one classroom beneath the chapel, but soon this became two classrooms, and as the church began to take shape, with an extensive flat roof, it became clear that this was the perfect place for kite-flying. I was so afraid that one of the children would fall off and die before time, that we began building the walls of the chapel sooner than expected. Our funds were running low and the building of St Antonio's took longer than expected, but once it was completed, Maria de Jesus went to Wetzlar in Germany to represent the parishioners and to express thanks. Maria also kept the spirit of the CEB's (Christian Based Communities) alive at St Antonio's, campaigning for better health and social facilities for women and children in the community.

In another community, the church was simply a shack in a favela. It was called Perpetuo Soccoro (Perpetual Succour) and it will always remain with me the community that had the most patience, not only with their children, but also in the construction of a new chapel. When I first arrived, the shack was being used as a place to celebrate the wakes of dead drug dealers. The church had become a no-go area. The only solution was to tear it down, and one woman, Palmira was a real fighter for the community. She was the catalyst for a new church to be built in its space. We had to be careful that we didn't block the sewage pipes underneath, which we did at first, and we had to be careful that when asking one of the old neighbours to move out of the stairway below, that he didn't vacate his place till the last minute before the bulldozers arrived, otherwise the drug gangs would move into his empty space. With funding again from Wetzlar, we were able to pay for him to move to a better place. After so many trials, we did it! It took years but we did it. We got a new church and Palmira was thrilled. I will always remember how the children climbed on the pews, shouted out during the services, and were just so dreadfully badly behaved. However, forty years later, that little church remains, and the 'dreadful' children are now the catechists, singers and church organisers. We really achieved the impossible there, but it is important not to think what might work, but to start doing something that may or may not work, and this is infinitely better than doing nothing at all.

No matter the triumphs, there was no escaping the violence in the favelas and I was particularly shaken by a murder in my house in Jardim Luzo in the community of St John the Baptist. I had been robbed a few times, but the armed criminals only wanted money, and I continued to develop my work as a priest focusing on the herbal and flower remedies. Fr Octavio, who had introduced me to herbal medicine had come to stay at my home while delivering a course to seminarians in the area. After he left, a parishioner from nearby St Marcos, who was thinking of joining an order of sisters, asked if she could stay at my home and cook for the day. She had brought a young boy with her. I was busy taking the course with Fr Octavio and agreed to her using my home while I was away. When I returned that night, she asked if they could stay overnight, and since Fr Octavio had left, I gave them his room. I also gave the young boy a sleeping bag. That night I awakened to terrible screams from the girl. The young boy had been slashed by someone who had come through the window and attacked him. He was covered in blood and I had to get him to hospital. I contacted St Marcos parish and the Parish Priest came to take the girl away. She was hysterical by this time. Some seminarians came to help me take the boy to hospital where he sadly died. I had to give a report to the police and to the Bishop and Provincial. The police contacted the girl and she had to explain why she was staying at my home, and who the boy was. It was a terrible incident, and I was so shaken by it, especially when I attended the boy's funeral. I could see the slash marks on his neck. There was never any reason discovered for his murder and the person that did it was never caught and for a long time after, it worried me that it would happen again, or that the assailant had really been targeting Fr Octavius or myself? I had made no enemies in the communities, but I felt uneasy for some time to come.

CHAPTER 13

Rest and Be Thankful

There was a growing trend in Brazil in the 1990s, and indeed internationally, for the Catholic Charismatic Movement to become part of the mass. This was a trend like Pentecostalism, where the congregations express their devotion through arrhythmic handclapping. I didn't belong to this movement, and I found that the excessive handclapping upset the melody and harmony of the traditional hymns. I always felt calm after saying mass, but when concelebrating with charismatic priests, I was left feeling frustrated. Why had I or congregations no choice in these new trends? Or perhaps the congregations related more to this type of worship than the western Roman style that I practised in Brazil.

Thankfully the herbal and floral remedies were unlikely to be disrupted by the charismatic craze. They had been around for thousands of years, and it was just a case of becoming more knowledgeable and experienced in how to make them available to those who needed them. Unhealthy diets and lifestyle of the poor is a global problem, but in Jardin Miriam, where there were 10 favelas and with only one health centre, the problems were exacerbated.

Part of the work of our clinic was to run courses in healthy eating and ensuring a balanced diet. We began to run courses to train health promoters, as well as exploring traditional and alternative medicines. We created a library and did research into the scientific properties of complementary medicines. I helped to train as many people in the community as I could in using a combination of remedies to improve mental and physical health. But I also had my spiritual responsibility to the community, developing their faith and administering the sacraments at the various stages of life.

One of the most important herbal remedies is tea, but the people in Jardim Miriam had no access to the tea plantations that I had seen growing in Minas Gerais. So we introduced a system where fresh tea leaves were transported to us and we extracted a tincture and produced micro-doses that became remedies for worms, gastro enteritis, constipation, coughs and sore throats. We also learned to make healing ointments that were miraculous in treating skin complaints. Bio-energy and treatments that strengthened the immune system were being introduced to Brazil at this time and I was very impressed with the work done by Sister Marialva who was instrumental in making it available within the communities. By the time Nossa Senhora Aparecida was celebrating its twenty-fifth anniversary, our clinic was well established with a wide range of therapies. We had many celebrations during this time, and I remember especially the 25-metre cake. It was made by each of the communities the parish served and when put together it was an amazing feat! After mass, where each of the communities brought symbols of their patron saints to be presented at the offertory, the magnificent cake was eaten in record time.

I had been in Jardim Miriam for several years now and it was time for a holiday. I needed some rest, and so it was lovely that I was invited to visit the family of my dear cousin Jack in Scotland. They were known as the McRobbie's in our family home in Dublin. My mother's elder sister Florence had gone to Scotland and married there. Her only son Jack was my cousin, and he was father to four daughters, my second cousins. My first port of call after meeting them were the mountains. I found myself being drawn to one of the main roads to the Isle of Skye known as the Rest and Be Thankful, when the gears on my bike broke and I had to drag it all the way up in the pouring rain. I learned that the name of this climb is in reference to the glorious view that can be found after the long arduous climb. After a week cycling around the Isle of Skye, I returned to the McRobbie family home where everyone remarked on my weather-beaten tanned look. After a shower, this look rapidly disappeared! Scotland is not the place to acquire a tan, but I did acquire a great connection with all my aunt Flo's family. You can read Florrie's story '*Howth*' written by Maura McRobbie available on Amazon. It's a story of eternal love, amid the tensions of religious intolerance in the mid twentieth century.

From Scotland I went to Switzerland and I felt so blessed to see the mountains, so colourful and picturesque in comparison with the brutal concrete and grey of Sao Paulo. I walked the Heilbrunner Mountain Weg. Hiking the summits from mountain to mountain, without ever having to descend, is wonderful and there are panoramic views from every angle. These were breath-taking. I had been invited to celebrate the wedding of Rainer and Michaela who had worked with me in Santarém. They arrived for their ceremony on a tandem. He in top hat and tails, and she in a flowing white dress riding on their bike. It was a great occasion, and, in my sermon, I compared marriage to the mountains. You cannot see the summit while you're undertaking the daily grind: the one step at a time along the mountain trail; but once you get to the top and look down at all that you have achieved together – it is an awe-inspiring spectacle. During this visit, I also met up with my missionary godmother Annelise Hoeller and we chatted and wished each other well before saying goodbye.

Back in Ireland, my family were waiting, and we had the usual celebrations and gatherings before it was time to head back to Brazil. My batteries had been recharged and I was no longer in need of rest, but I was thankful for all the good times and welcomes I had received. It wasn't long after my return that I heard the sad news of Annalise's death in Wetzlar in Germany. She had been like a second mother to me, passing my name onto influential priests and parishes who would later help fund the construction of so many community churches that are still in Jardim Miriam today. From my years as a seminarian, I was so fortunate to have had her in my life. On her memorial card it was written:

"I tell you all, goodbye, because I went ahead of you; sooner or later you will follow me."

Instead of flowers at her graveside, where she was buried beside her husband, she asked that donations be sent to me in Brazil. I celebrated mass for her in Nossa Senhora Aparecida, where all the parishioners felt they knew her from my stories. She sacrificed herself tirelessly for her Christian faith and I missed her dearly. May She Rest in Peace.

The Phytotherapy Courses and BioEnergy Groups were going well in all the communities, and we were interested in combining some physical exercise into our programme of wellbeing. Tai Chi was underway in many areas and I was interested in introducing Lian Gong, a Chinese form of Tai Chi that is accompanied by music. We used the main square in Jardim Miriam to do the exercises and church halls. Many people came to these and soon the parish councils organised training for teachers in Lian Gong to be undertaken in health clinics and centres. And for some reason I wasn't content with all the focus on healthy living, but I wanted to continue my theatre groups that had been so successful in Santarém. But this required work and dedication, not just from myself, the producer, but from the actors, the scene builders, the costume makers and of course the stage builders. When we were casting, the person that played Jesus in the Passion Play, as well as being the centre of the action, he had to be strong to help assemble and disassemble the whole production. It was a team effort. On Good Friday, the day would start early with over thirty people constructing the stage until noon. The celebration of the Liturgy began at 3pm and lasted for two to three hours with Jesus leading the procession all through the streets of Jardim Miriam. Later we walked over to the stage and began to prepare for the performance. It began with Pilate's condemnation of Jesus and ended with the Crucifixion. Once it was over and the people gone, it was time then to start dismantling the stage and equipment. Thank goodness for Fernando who came with his truck to transport it away, all before 1am. When they came back to the chapel house happy but exhausted, all I had to give them was the brandy used for the Bach remedies. It worked every time! Over the years our Passion Play went from strength to strength, and it was fulfilling to see so many people work together in harmony in something that gave so much pleasure to the community. As a young seminarian I never knew that I would be scripting, directing, lighting and producing an annual Passion Play. For these wonderful moments I will always be grateful. But life in Jardim Miriam wasn't always fun and games.

CHAPTER 14

Forgive me for I Have Sinned

One day when I was on duty at Nossa Senhora Aparecida, a stranger came to the door wishing to speak to a priest. Theresa, my faithful 'shield' asked what it was in connection with, and he replied gravely,

"I've got a confession to make," so she showed him into my office. He didn't begin in the traditional way, but by the following: "Reverend Father, I owe some guys some money. If I don't pay them immediately, they are going to kill me. That is why I need your help to pay the debt." And he placed a 38 calibre revolver on my desk, taking one bullet out at a time until he had them all lined up in a perfectly straight row. He went on to persuade me that it was my duty as a priest to preserve his life, not to let him die, and he asked me for 189 Reais which immediately I recognised was not a huge sum. As he menacingly began placing the bullets back in the revolver, I said I would go and get the money. I silently headed to the room where the safe was located and removed 190 Reais, I returned to the man, who by this time had the revolver loaded and pointing at me as I entered the office. I said quietly and calmly to him that I had the money and if I gave it to him, I wouldn't call the police, as long as he agreed never to come back. He lowered the gun and swiftly took the money and left. As he went out the front door I said:

"Go in peace and don't sin anymore." Poor Theresa didn't know what was happening and when I told her she was terrified. She promised that the next time a stranger knocked the door of the house asking for confession, she would point them in the direction of the chapel, before or after mass.

There were other incidences where at gunpoint I was asked for the keys of my car when I was just arriving home. I dropped to my knees faking a heart attack, but the guy wasn't at all concerned and as I lay on the ground, he turned me around, whipped the keys from my pocket and the watch from my wrist. My car was later found with the radio removed. Another time when a fellow priest and I arrived home from a meeting, two guys jumped on us and locked us in the ground floor toilet, saying they would shoot us if we tried to get out. I tried to telephone the police on my mobile, but they heard me and came back ordering me to give them my car keys. (Luckily, I had quickly hidden my phone in the toilet paper box so they didn't get it.) But by this time, they had ransacked the house and taken the TV that we had just bought. Then they took the CD player, tape recorder and kitchen equipment and put them in my car, but the alarm went off and the key got stuck in the ignition. They were unable to make their escape in my car, leaving half the stolen items behind them. The TV set they had managed to put into a van they had brought with them.

There was another inconsequential shooting around this time, on the outskirts of Jardim Miriam known as Diadema. This was an extremely poor area that again had a shack as a church. Prayers and celebrations were organised by Sister Anna Maria of the St Joseph of Chambery Sisters. The shack was owned by Zé de Porco who was a pig keeper. I asked him if we could buy the shack from him so that we could build something more permanent and suitable for worship on the site. With the money he would be able to buy something better and more spacious for his pigs. He agreed and I paid him before beginning the reconstruction. The sewers were a problem, diverting them from under the building, but the council became involved and helped improve the drainage. This was necessary because the area tended to flood each year. The walls were plywood which meant they curved in the humidity, and we needed to build new steps to access the church, but slowly but surely, we got there. Once we were finished, Sister Anna Maria encouraged hundreds of people to attend services from all over Diadema. The church was called St Judas and was very close to a landfill site and in order for people to come, they had to manoeuvre steep steps and walk past plywood makeshift homes with no roads or pavements. The community had been formed long before the sewage and drainage improvements were done, and it was always heartening to see members of the community volunteering to help the builders finish the church. Sister Anna Maria organised such beautiful services there. It felt like heaven inside when outside was grinding poverty and hardship. It shouldn't have been a surprise to me, but I was so upset to find Zé do Porco dead one day near to the church in one of the sewers, shot at point blank range, probably by those who wanted to steal the money he got from selling his shack. The police never found out who was responsible for his murder. Once again, I prayed that his murderers would be forgiven and not sin again.

At the same time, it was important to breathe new life into the pastoral work of Nossa Senhora Aparecida. Jardim Miriam was an area that seemed almost forgotten by the authorities and yet there were 72,000 inhabitants. The clinic we ran had about 150 – 200 people passing through each week, and we had more than 70 volunteers acting as receptionists, producing micro doses and creams, providing massage therapies and a programme of physical activities throughout the year. Our work was about preventative medicine, before depression or disease took hold and before prescription drugs or indeed illegal drugs became addictive. Our clinic provided alternative remedies to many of life's common ailments, many of which were exacerbated by living in extreme poverty surrounded by robberies and violence. We didn't claim to run a medical health centre, even though there was no such thing in Jardim Miriam in those days; and we didn't claim to ward off demons as there were other churches that veered in this direction. What we did was administer hope through affordable and effective herbal treatments, dietary guidance, and exercise.

We were responsible in our efforts and if a clinically sick person came to us where our remedies would have little effect, we would refer them to doctors or psychologists who were specialists in their field. Over the years we treated thousands of patients and trained many volunteers who are still practising today. We had our enemies who would have preferred us to be shut down, but by persevering and seeing Christ in all those we treated, some deeply in despair, we felt we were putting our faith into action. When Father Manfred visited us from Wetzlar in Germany, and saw the extent of our work, he asked if exchange visits could be arranged between our parish and Wetzlar. In the first exchange, Maria de Jesus from the community of St Antonio, Theresa the parish secretary and Leda, a chatechist were selected to fly to Germany and share the results of their work in the parish of Nossa Senhora Aparecida. Father Manfred had so much experience as a parish priest, and as well as helping us financially, he breathed new life into our work, and made us feel so valued.

And finally, one of the strongest images that is embedded in my mind, is of this extraordinary community in Jardim Miriam, working together to improve their church. A new mezzanine floor was needed in the church to provide additional space. A group of voluntary parishioners, men, young and old, came to build this. They mixed the cement, and with their bare hands they laid the new floor. It was heavy, dirty work in a very hot climate and their hands were covered in welts, but the laughter and camaraderie as they stopped for lunch and were fed by the women of the community, will live with me forever. There was something spiritual about the way they worked in a united team. The feeling that I had been the catalyst for good in the face of great adversity, was a potent drug, and I was hooked.

CHAPTER 15

Climb Every Mountain

As the world began to prepare for the Millennium, I began to prepare for my 25th anniversary as a priest. I would go to Dublin and celebrate with family and friends, and I would have many masses and celebrations in Jardim Miriam. It was 1997 and these were the closing chapters of what had been an incredible century. In the late summer of that year, three distinguished figures who had helped to alleviate the suffering of the poor and shed an international light on their plight, died. I found it strange that they passed away within a few weeks of each other. I imagined them having a great celebration in heaven, their life's work done, they had truly earned their wings.

The first was Herbert de Souza Betinho, a sociologist and activist who was not religious, but he was an impressive humanitarian and a symbol of hope for all those who hungered. In 1992 when he discovered that 32 million Brazilians, (almost a quarter of the population) suffered acute hunger, he mobilised professionals, workers, and others to fund-raise for the dispossessed. In 1994 he started an annual campaign called "Christmas without Hunger" and he launched a movement for Ethics in Politics. During the

1990s, when the AIDS/HIV epidemic began, he set up controlled blood banks through the Brazilian Interdisciplinary Aids Association to ensure the infection was not spread further. He campaigned for those afflicted with AIDS to be treated with dignity and worked to have educational programmes that lessened the stigma attached to those who were rapidly dehumanised and pauperised by the disease.

Betinho's life had not been easy from the start. He was a haemophiliac and relied on blood transfusions to survive. In 1964 during the Military Regime, he was exiled because of his movement: "Acao Popular" that mobilised the poor into challenging their disadvantages openly with the government. Even though this was a non-Marxist movement, it was frowned on by the regime and it was safer for Betinho to leave Brazil. In 1970, once all those exiled were given amnesty, he returned and continued his work with the poor. It is said that his eyes shone like "lighthouses that guided and illuminated ways to be trod." He died in August 1997 after complications from a blood transfusion. Prizes and awards have been set up in his honour and a bridge in Rio de Janeiro is named after him.

Not long after his death, another international figure, who had shone the same light on those suffering from AIDS and had visited

Brazil in 1991, died in a car crash in Paris. This was Diana, Princess of Wales and her humanitarian legacy was well documented at the end of the twentieth century. She had visited Mother Theresa's Hospital in the Bronx in New York in the summer of 1997. Mother Theresa was feeling poorly but welcomed her and they walked the streets of the Bronx together. The two shared a bond and their mission in life, like Betinho's, had been to shine a light on those who suffered in order that governments would act. Diana died on 31st of August 1997 and Mother Theresa passed away less than a week later on the 5th September. Three distinguished people destined to party in heaven in that Indian summer of 1997. Before Betinho died, he foresaw the potential of the internet, that was in its infancy then, as having the immense power to raise funds for charity. And he was right.

As I had now spent most of my life in Brazil, I found I felt more Brazilian than Irish. The Catholic church that I believed in was the one that Pope Francis speaks so clearly of today: to be a priest it is important to be engaged in the political, social and economic problems of the community, as well as the spiritual. Each are interlinked, and many people's spiritual lives are affected by their social and economic situations.

One of my friends, Sister Edel of the SSpS, whom I had kept in touch with since my days as a seminarian, and who continued her work in Laupheim in Germany had travelled to Ireland to join in my silver jubilee celebrations. We then returned to Germany together by way of the ferry to Cherbourg in France. A rock 'n' roll band was playing Elvis and the Beatles songs, and we danced on board until we dropped. In Germany that summer, as well as my daily language lessons, I climbed as many mountains as possible. Laupheim is in the Stuttgart area, which is in the Bavarian region and is surrounded by mountains, so there are so many to choose from. Sister Edel climbed some with me, and others she left me to conquer alone. She also organised a wonderful Mozart Mass at St John the Baptist Church in Oberstdorf, where we were given special seats near the choir and orchestra and I cried all the way through it. It was the feast of Our Lady of the Assumption, the 15th of August and I was overcome with appreciation and thanksgiving for my life. It was 38 years since I had started that job in Arnotts in Dublin, and 32 years since I had joined the Divine Word Missionaries.

Not long after, I left to go to visit Sister Beth and her family in Kitzbuhel in Austria. There were more mountains to climb, and these were higher than the Bavarian ones. Sometimes we organised Bergmessen where mass was celebrated at the top of the mountain. Many people joined in these climbs and musicians accompanied us and played at the summit. I enjoyed these open-air masses so much. There was great company during the climb and thanksgiving on the mountain top, surrounded by the peaks that almost touched the universe. I always felt a sense of Greatness here. The sharing of bread and wine, the oneness, and the feeling of encountering Christ. These masses always deepened my faith and connection with God.

Psalm 8: *"Your name Lord is so beautiful. You live in heaven up there. Even small children know that you are defeating the enemy. Looking at the sky that you made, I see the stars, I see the moon, and I understand that man is worth a lot, because you did everything for him. Smaller than the angels, but full of grace and value, you received power and strength of everything to win and dominate. The oxen and the sheep in the corrals and the cattle that graze, the fish of the sea and the birds in the fields and everything that cuts the air and the water."*

It wasn't long after my Silver Jubilee trip home to Europe that Sister Edel and her colleagues from Germany came to visit Brazil, and as well as showing them all the tourist highlights in Rio de Janeiro, I had to take them to the mountains in Sao Paulo. The Pico das Agulhas Negras (Black Needle) is the fifth highest mountain in Brazil (2791 metres) and is located in the Itatiaia National Park. It lies on the border of Minas Gerais, Rio de Janeiro and Sao Paulo. On our journey there, (which took me back to when I had first worked in Brazil,) I made sure they tasted the delicious cheese bread (Pao de Queijo) made on the spot, and served with warm, fresh coffee. What a delight. There is no other taste like it! From the little shops en route, we bought cheese and honey to take back with us. Once we were at the gate of the National Park we had to park the car, and then we began the climb. It is not for beginners, and although I'd climbed it myself on several occasions, on this day, we were content to do 5km of the ascent, and take in the view of the Black Needles from afar. Once again, I felt my closeness to God on this climb, even although we didn't make the summit.

One time before this, when I was alone and climbing this same mountain, I remembered how lucky I had been. With the mist descending, I had parked my car at what looked like a trail that would lead me up to a higher part of the mountain. In fact, it was an animal trail, and it soon dipped down and meandered in an entirely different direction. I should have turned back then, but I felt I knew in which direction the hostel was, where I was staying the night. However, along with the mist, night descended rapidly, and it soon became clear that I was lost. There were no mobile phones then, and I only had a cannister of water with me. I was kicking myself, I should have obeyed the mountain rules, and stuck to the official routes. My legs were torn and scratched by thornbushes and as I began to despair, I was sure I heard jaguars lurking in the undergrowth. But hadn't someone told me if you can hear them, you are safe from them? It's when there's silence.... that's when they strike. It began to drizzle and my legs were burning with pain. I collected some of my urine to soothe my wounds and it had an instant effect. The moon began to rise slowly, and with it my spirits. I began to see what looked like a trail, and as I placed one foot in front of the other, under the moonlight, the forest trail became clearer. In the distance, soon, the hostel where I had booked to stay overnight, came into view. It was 5am in the morning by this time. I had parked my car at 3pm in the afternoon for what should have been a two-hour climb. As I fell into bed, I was grateful that I'd found my way back safely but irritated at my lack of respect for the rules of the mountains. It would never happen again.

CHAPTER 16

Home

Norberto, from Germany, arrived in Sao Paulo as a newly ordained priest to help serve at Nossa Senhora de Aparecida and like me, he made Brazil his home. Every church has at its core a mission to encourage parishioners to attend mass, to take part in the liturgy and to receive the sacraments. The best way to start is through baptism and then to encourage children in their spiritual journey by supporting and welcoming parents. This is becoming more and more difficult, especially amongst young working parents who find little time to teach their children about Christ and the gospels, let alone to come to mass. In some countries, it is the school's responsibility, in other countries, schools are secular, and it is the church's responsibility. Whatever the case, each parish needs to have catechists to help share the message, and there needs to be priests to lead and inspire. Norberto was adept at working with parents, training catechists, and working with children. He had no trouble holding their attention and he would gather them around, entertaining them with his interpretations of the gospel stories.

Norberto and I became great friends and we shared a love of the mountains. He was German and his father visited him several times in Sao Paulo and we would go climbing together. His father was too frail to climb mountains, but instead he would take photographs of plants, nature and the tropical vegetation. Norberto had a great relationship with his old father and he took great care of him each time he visited. His father may have lacked energy to climb mountains, but he made up for this after dinner when he could talk and talk.

When I left Nossa Senhora Aparecida in 2005, Norberto took over as parish priest and I always knew the parish was in safe hands. He had a firm grasp of theology, but he also had a way of communicating the more difficult aspects in a simple, clear way. He was able to deliver courses at every level, and it was fun as well as enlightening to work with him. Norberto's small modest room was full of books, not novels or magazines, but books on theology, sociology and science. He lived humbly, without much money, but with what he had, he always shared, especially the pizzas we ate on Sundays after mass. He was highly esteemed within the Divine Word community, and he was well liked by all the parishioners. While supporting the poorest in society, and preaching for justice, he never put his name to any political party, or used the pulpit to encourage support of political leaders. I considered Norberto a true friend and colleague, and it came as no surprise to me when several years later, I was asked to write a reference for him to become a Bishop. In 2021 he was appointed by Pope Francis as Bishop in a place where I was to give courses in Bach Flower Remedies in Ji Paraná in the state of Rondônia.

As the new millennium dawned, I was ready for an extended sabbatical and there were plenty of courses to choose from. I knew where my interests lay and in which direction I was going. I set my sights on Bach Flower Remedy courses in Oxford in the UK and in California in the USA. My trip back to Europe began in the north of Scotland, in Elgin where my friend Juliette and her husband lived. They had been inspirational in my use of floral remedies in my parish and I was keen to visit them in Scotland. Elgin is near Inverness, and it was cold even in midsummer, but I was made to feel so at home with them, especially during their musical evenings performed by Juliette's talented family.

One of Juliette's friends visited while I was there. Her name was Jo and she was from London. She was an excellent swimmer and challenged us all to a competition. At 75 years of age she was off like a torpedo when we swam at the baths in Elgin, and of course, she won. When I got to Oxford, I was staying at the Salesian's house and Jo kindly drove me there from London. Her mother was in a nursing home in Oxford and she visited her weekly. I discovered a magnificent swimming pool behind the College and each week Jo and I had a swim, and of course each time she was off like a shot, hammering out lengths as though she was an Olympian. I was so impressed with her energy and that she was always willing to pick me up and drop me off at Heathrow Airport on numerous occasions. I was sad to hear of her death during lockdown in 2020, but happy to know that she would have her final wish of being laid to rest in the country church where she had lived as a child when she was evacuated during the war. Her memoir, "Waiting for the Bluebirds" describes this experience evocatively and is written in her pseudonym, June Matthews and is available on Amazon.

In Oxford at the Bach Remedy Centre, I found the weather warmer than in Elgin, and the course was interesting and practical. The delegates were multi-disciplinary, some came with a background in holistic therapies, others, like me in herbal and preventative medicines. I had time to visit my friend Joanne, from my seminarian days. She was married now to a yachtsman called Tom and we went sailing together around the south coast. I had no fear whatsoever under the capable hands of Tom, but as the yacht banked and listed, I found it a different experience from my balmy riverboat days up the Amazon. We visited the New Forest and I was enthralled by the ancient oak trees and the magnificent dappled light not far from inner city London. However, seeing all the ancient oak trees in the New Forest only brought home to me the decimated oak trees in Ireland, plundered by the English to increase their shipping fleets to fight Ireland, France and Spain. This was when England ruled the waves and as the anthem goes, 'they never ever would be slaves' – but surely they made slaves of other nations? I didn't want England to bring out the worst in me, but sometimes my train of thought would go this way. The destruction of another country's natural habitat to boost the wealth and power of another. It's the same story as in Brazil.

It was time for me to go to California and I hoped for a better frame of mind. The theology courses there were excellent and we read and discussed Leonardo Boff's teachings on 'Creation':

"Humanity stands at a crossroads. We can either continue a path towards increasing exploitation, inequality, and destruction – threatening both human civilization and the entire web of life upon which we depend – or, as the Earth Charter reminds us, we may choose instead to 'form a global partnership to care for Earth and one another." His work was validated by Pope Francis in his Laudato Si Encyclical Letter in 2015, and Boff, a Liberation Theologist and former priest, is now Professor Emeritus of Ethics, Philosophy of Religion, and Ecology at the Rio de Janeiro State University. He also received the Right Livelihood Award for his "his inspiring insights and practical work to help people realise the links between human spirituality, social justice and environmental stewardship."

In California I quickly made an impact as the Irish/Brazilian priest. I was pleased that everyone could understand my accent, because one of the course delegates was Australian, and the Americans couldn't understand a word he said. I could understand him perfectly and he helped me so much with my technology skills as emails and word-processing were in their infancy then. However, no matter how he tried, no one could understand him. They looked to me to translate for him, so I became known as the Irish/Brazilian priest who translated Australian into English! Another way in which I made an impression was when I broke my shoulder after a bike fall. I needed physiotherapy and one of the course delegates, a reflexologist, massaged and soothed my aching muscles while I prescribed her herbal remedies to appease her ailments.

A beautiful American woman was the course leader. She was tall and serene with a calm and detached air. I didn't realise until her partner joined us for dinner, that they were from the LGBT community. They were campaigning for women priests in a peaceful crusade. They felt the church was wasting time and losing so many of the faithful by not appointing deaconesses and training female priests. I found I was not at home; not because I didn't believe in women priests, or that I was against LGBT values, but that my direction was in empowering the poor to become more knowledgeable about their rights and providing them with the skills to work together to obtain safer water systems, improved health care, and a better quality of life. These were my drivers. This is what motivated me, so while I respected their campaign, I realised I was on a different path. I left California with my arm in a sling to return to Germany. I was met by Sr Edel at the railway station, and I felt completely at home.

CHAPTER 17

Urine and Clay Therapy

At this stage in my life, I was interested in its efficacy and that is why I had come to Germany as I was attending the International Urine Therapy Conference. I learned that Urine therapy is not new, that ancient cultures in Asia have used it in many ways during the ages. It is important first to detoxify the body and to eat natural foods rather than processed. Water is essential, drinking at least 1 litre of water to every 30 kilos of weight. Then urine can be used with water to cook vegetables, but it cannot be used to cook meat, so in a meat-eating country like Brazil, I knew it was never going to catch on. However, as an antiseptic on wounds or as a skin treatment, leaving it on the skin for at least thirty minutes and then showering, can make the skin soft and silky. I wasn't sure if this would be something I could encourage back in Sao Paulo, but I was pleased to hear that the next International Urine Therapy Conference was to be held in Brazil in 2003.

Once back in Brazil, I attended a Health Congress in Quito in Ecuador that was a precursor to the Brazilian conference. It was here that I heard the news that Lula De Silva had been successful in the first round of presidential elections. I was thrilled. Lula would ensure that the poor and marginalised would at last be able to eat three times a day, and he would inject millions into social programmes to help ease social inequalities. His presidency was to last two terms and span eight years. Flying into Quito Airport, the descent was steep and tricky within a very mountainous region, and of course, when I saw the mountains, I just had to climb them!

The day before the Congress began, I set off with my metal sticks, to tackle a mountain that lay behind the SVD home and I followed the trail that led up to it. On my descent, I took another trail and entered unwittingly into wild dog territory. As soon as they got my scent, these abandoned dogs came after me, and the leader of the pack began to attack me with snarling teeth. I struck its nose with the metal poles, and this held it back, but the others surrounded me. I began to back away from them, stabbing at them with my sticks, until I fell over and rolled down onto the trail below. That's when they stopped their attack as I was now out with their territory. But I was badly shaken, my knee was twisted, and I was covered in scratches and bruises. That evening, I developed flu symptoms and couldn't stop shivering. As well as that, I needed physiotherapy on my knee to mobilise. I wasn't the healthiest of specimens on the first day of the Health Congress. However, it was an excellent conference with so many aspects of alternative remedies and therapies discussed with medics from all over Latin America. I learned sadly however, that many doctors, while supporting the use of alternative therapies, would lose their licenses if they prescribed or advised their use. As well as urine therapy and fasting, the Congress also highlighted the use of bio thermals to balance the circulation through clay and steam baths and an emphasis on a plant based chemical free diet. There were many testimonies of people suffering from cancer, diabetes and AIDS using these treatments to help alleviate their symptoms. Western thinking at this time resisted all the scientifically based evidence, however, twenty years later, fasting and diet-based treatments for diabetes and cancer are frequently recommended. By the end of the Congress, a support network was set up to ensure alternative therapies were not dismissed out of hand and I had made many contacts to bring back to the Conference in Brazil.

I was introduced to clay therapy at the Congress through a French therapist, Dr Jade Allegre from Paris. Clay therapy is sometimes called geotherapy and many are familiar with clay treatments that are applied externally for many skin problems. It forms the basis for many beauty treatments such as face masks and cleansers and it is first recorded as a treatment both internally and externally in Chinese medicine. Clay can act as an anti-inflammatory when applied to the skin, and when taken internally, mixed in a glass of water and left overnight, it can solve gastric problems such as dysentery and diarrhoea. Jade was passionate about clay treatments and in France, where clay therapy is far more advanced than the rest of the world, she is a well-known guest on TV programmes. However, she has also been threatened many times by the laboratories, for her work with these "treatments". On leaving the Congress, I was inspired by Jade and the vast array of alternative remedies, and I felt, with a little bit of fasting and prayer, it was easy to become super healthy!

Back at the parish in Jardim Miriam, things weren't going so well. It was beset with problems of the terrestrial kind: bills to be paid, the roof needing maintained and a multitude of other parish issues. I felt my strengths lay in the liturgy, in delivering the sacraments and in herbal and floral treatments. There were endless meetings on where our priorities lay, whether in pastoral work, in health and wellbeing, or in financial fund-raising. It was not an easy time, but I took strength in the fact that we were celebrating ten years of our health clinics, where the problems, (created by living in a huge inner city,) such as loneliness, unemployment, drug abuse, vandalism and violence, could be discussed and grievances aired. Beth Bruno, who represented a group called Semente (Seed), came to our parish and she was instrumental in teaching and training us in how to use healing herbal remedies using our own collected flowers and herbs.

This meant we no longer relied on manufactured remedies and could produce our own.

Beth and I then travelled to Ji Parana, a city in Rondônia in north-western Brazil to attend seminars and workshops to teach about Bach Flower remedies. Ji Parana was a fast growing, disorganised city founded in 1977. It is located in the interior of Rondônia in the middle of the Amazon rainforest, to the south west of Santarém. Many of the population are illiterate and few complete higher education. Resources are limited and sanitation is poor. When we visited we observed much deforestation of the rainforest taking place in this region, using illegally built roads extending northwards to Bolivia. It was so sad to see this happening, especially as the Amazon is the stronghold for medicinal plants and relies on the layers of the eco system – the canopy of trees that provides food and shelter for all other species – to produce plants and vegetation that have the potential to eliminate diseases. When I was in this part of the world, it made me feel more committed than ever to the belief that herbal medicine must no longer be consigned, as was the case in history, to religious orders: monks and sisters in their monasteries and convents, but they must be recognised internationally and given the credit they deserve and we must work together to preserve the Amazon rainforests if we are to protect generations to come.

The Urine Therapy Conference of Brazil took place in 2003 and it was attended by a vast variety of international therapists. I was there as a therapist as well as a priest, so I ensured that masses were said and thanksgivings made for our health and for our ability to share our knowledge and care with others. Solutions were found to the repairs required to the parish in Jardim Miriam and there were lots of weddings and baptisms to celebrate: actors from my plays were marrying actresses; and one of our priests who was a student with me, was graduating and taking up his first post as a lawyer, going to work in the Amazon, and hopefully legislating to protect the rainforests. I was feeling satisfied with my parish, the circle of life and the fruits of my labour. I was sixty years old, and it was time for me to renew my faith and take a closer look at myself. I began to plan my Pilgrimage to Santiago de Compostela in Spain.

CHAPTER 18

Wilkommen, Bienvenidos, Welcome

I didn't know what to expect when I embarked on the pilgrimage to Santiago de Compostela in Galicia in north-western Spain. It is usual for pilgrims to walk but as I had torn my tendon from over-training in ill-fitting shoes, I decided that I should go by bike and I bought myself a new one for the occasion. (It was a treat for my sixtieth birthday and incidentally, I still have the same bike twenty years later sitting outside my back yard here in Sao Paulo.) In order to take it to Spain, I would have to dismantle it for the plane, and then reconfigure it once I landed. I had always wanted to do this pilgrimage since I was young. I knew it was a challenging route – thirty days by foot and 750km to cover from the start in France – fifteen days by bike. I wanted to do it alone, not in a group, to deepen my faith and to have an encounter with myself.

The story of Santiago is that Saint James, an apostle of Jesus, was buried in a small forest in Galicia in the days of the Roman Empire. Almost 800 years later, discovered by Christians, this site became the goal of one of the most well-travelled routes in Christendom including those of Jerusalem and Rome. The Jacobean pilgrimage

(Tiago – is James in Latin) reached its peak in the 11th and 12th centuries but was almost forgotten by the 18th century. However, it was rediscovered in the 20th century and especially in Brazil, when the writer, Paulo Coelho highlighted it in his book 'The Pilgrimage'. He described it as a way of discovering your own path – "the extraordinary is to be found in the everyday ordinary." This is precisely what I wanted to encounter, from the everyday 'ordinary', to discover the 'extraordinary'.

I began on the feast day of St José de Anchieta, who was the Spanish missionary who had worked in the Amazon, using theatre and performance as a way of sharing the Gospels. He was my role model for much of the missionary work I had done in Santarém, and I felt he was my guiding light. I arrived via Madrid then Pamplona Airports where I was taken to Roncesvalles in the Navarre region of northern Spain. This is where I would begin the pilgrimage. It was so pleasant to be welcomed by SVD brother Antonio, and Miguel and his wife who would take me to the hostel and help me get rid of some of the things I didn't need. These would be sent on to Santiago and Madrid for me to retrieve later. As I arrived early, before the hostel was opened, I began reassembling my bike only to find that the gears had been nudged out of synchronisation during the flight, and the brakes were rubbing. I would still be able to ride it until I got to a bicycle repair specialist, but I wouldn't be able to go at speed. I was careful as well to read all the regulations that that were required of cyclists going on the pilgrimage as these were different to the walkers. The hostel at Roncesvalles was high up in the Pyrenees and it was like a beautiful convent or monastery. They were repairing the roof, replacing some of the wooden beams with what looked like yellow pine, and the smell of this fresh wood was simply wonderful. I ate in a restaurant in the town: a special menu for pilgrims at the start of their journey for just 7 euros. I had delicious soup, trout, bread and wine. This was followed by prayers, vespers and mass. I slept so peacefully that night in anticipation of the 50km I would begin the next morning.

The first part of my route took me back towards Pamplona where my flight had landed two days before. I was delighted to have arrived at a church just in time for 12 noon mass and I carefully padlocked my bike, with my two large saddle bags, inside the church grounds, behind the gates. After mass I thought I'd take a short stroll into the town for coffee – and I was luxuriating in the taste of Spanish coffee, trying to work out whether it was the water that made it different from Brazil, or perhaps it could be the quality of beans they used (although I was sure the best beans would be Brazilian). Anyway, time ran away with me, and as I made my way back to the church, the gates were locked, and my bike and saddle bags firmly off limits. I went straight to the parish house and rang the bell, but I was told by the housekeeper that I'd need to wait until the next mass at 6pm that evening when the priest would open the gates. I was distraught, I couldn't wait six hours. I needed to complete my 50 km and be at my destination by evening. So I persisted. Finally, the parish priest appeared mumbling and grumbling and I'm sure saying 'I don't need to do this you know! Disturbing my lunch.' Anyway, I got my bike and I was back on the road.

I found that the tracks were full of tree roots and were hilly and weren't suitable for cycling, so I made my way by road. I arrived at Cizur Menor by mid-afternoon and I soon found a hostel with a church nearby. I was very moved by the Pilgrim's Prayer I found in this church and I made sure I said it every day:

Pilgrim's Prayer

Father I put myself in your hands.
Do to me what you want,
Whatever it is, I give you thanks.
I am willing to do anything, I accept everything.
As long as your Will be completed in me
And all your creatures.
I no longer desire, Father, I trust my being.
I give you all the love I am capable of because I love you
And I need to give myself to you.

I put myself in your hands, without limitations, without measure
With infinite confidence, because you are my Father.
Amen

My first day hadn't been too bad I reflected as I made myself a herbal tea from the portable pharmacy I had brought with me. The yellow leaves were as fragrant as the gorse bushes I had cycled past earlier. I ate in the only restaurant in Cizur Menor and was served vegetable soup with chunks of ham in it, even although I had asked for a vegetarian soup. Maybe I hadn't made myself understood. This was followed by fish and bread washed down with copious rioja. When I returned to the hostel, I was upset to discover that I had forgotten my bible and daily readings, but I said my own prayers and put my faith and trust in God just as the Pilgrim's Prayer recommended. The guy next to me snored the whole night. It wasn't me, honest!

The next day was beautiful and with only 36km to cycle to reach Estella, I was told by the hostel warden, that this would be one of the easier days. He advised me to take an alternative route which he said was the best one. I did this but found that the sun was beating down and although I am used to high temperatures and mountain climbing, this was entirely different when my gears and brakes let me down, and I had to push the bike with two heavy saddle bags and a backpack uphill. This was exhausting and the only thing that kept me going was the thought of the welcome I would receive at the SVD house in Estella. Antonio, who had met me at the Airport had described its exact location to me, and said it was so obvious, the first on the right as I entered Estella, and that I couldn't miss it. I visualised a cool shower and delicious food awaiting me with my fellow brothers, as I continued the uphill struggle with my bikes and baggage. However, as I had taken a different route into the town, (the one recommended by the warden) I completely missed the right-hand turn and ended up at a hostel filled to the brim with pilgrims speaking in a babble of indistinguishable languages. The warden told me that I had passed the SVD house by about twenty minutes. Without an ounce of energy left in my body, I accepted his welcome for the night, and put my faith in his hospitality. In town I devoured a whole loaf of bread and a few beers before searching for someone who could repair my bike. I was impressed by the mechanic I found who did a marvellous job and refused to be paid after two hours work. He knew I was a pilgrim on the way to Compostela and he was full of admiration for me. He asked only for a prayer. I paid him nonetheless and I prayed for him too. That night I thought of the welcomes I'd received along the way and was grateful. I didn't realise then that I wouldn't receive many more welcomes like these in the days to follow.

CHAPTER 19

Casting Off

Fifteen days on a bike on the Camino, the highway or freeway, in high temperatures, is bound to test anyone's patience and I suppose you are bound to discover some inner emotions you haven't confronted before. Maybe it's because you don't have a home. On a pilgrimage you depend completely on others, on strangers. You start off the journey with all the props that keep you going in life; the things you like; your simple pleasures; the things you wear; the herbal drinks that pep you up; the daily readings that keep you on track. I suppose nowadays with technology today's pilgrims will take their iphones; their podcasts; their earphones and be able to dip into what interests them on the journey. However, what I found on the Camino was that I had to cast off all life's props one by one. This is something the pilgrimage taught me: to give it up; to give possessions held near and dear away; to do without them. To travel light and to value the simplest pleasures as if they were the real treasures in life.

The first things I had to cast off were the excessive kilos I was carrying, whether it was clothes, or books, or whatever. Carrying my bike up all those hills made me certain I was carrying far too much, and I would never make it, so I posted several packages onto the SVD centre in Madrid so that I could pick up later. That lightened my load somewhat and I cycled onwards. The next hostel at Nagéra was interesting. As I arrived early, I was told to return at 8pm to be allocated a bed for the night. I was able to wash and dry some clothes, and I went for an early evening meal. A large bottle of rioja was placed on the table, and as no other pilgrims turned up while I was there, I managed to drink the whole bottle! I still don't know how I managed to do this, but when I cycled back to the hostel, I was told that I would be sleeping in a sports centre that was about a kilometre away. When I got there, I discovered that I would be sleeping on the floor, and furthermore, in my wish to lighten my load, I had left my sleeping bag in Estella. I had to go back to the hostel and ask for blankets and a mat, before returning to the sports centre. Just as well I was on my bike, as I was too tipsy to walk, and of course, I slept like a log even although the guy next to me snored even louder than the guy the night before.

Things didn't always run smoothly. On one part of the journey, where I was really looking forward to arriving and having a shower before finding somewhere for dinner, I was given a frosty reception. The warden took great exception to my saddle bags. He said they were dusty and too big to be brought into the dormitory. He gave me a plastic bag and told me to leave my saddle bags and bike in a shed and bring only my necessary items back with me otherwise I wouldn't be admitted to the hostel. I was so angry. Not just with the warden and his rules, but angry to be parted from my meagre possessions. I had become so attached to them. I had to dig deep that night and let go of my fury, but soon I was showering and washing my clothes and preparing for the next day.

Another place along the way that symbolically demonstrated the 'casting off' of old ways for the newly transformed ways, was The Iron Cross at Foncebadón. This cross had been fixed into the ground on a long oak mast. It was thought to be the original location of a Roman shrine, and through time had become a notable place of worship for Medieval pilgrims. The tradition was for pilgrims, as they passed, to place a stone or rock at the base, creating a mountain around the cross. However, many pilgrims also used it as a site to cast off their worn shoes, garments of clothing; old bits and pieces and as a result, it looked such an eyesore. There was nothing spiritual or transformational here, just a bit of a wasteland. It was time to move on and I began to recognise that I was entering 'negative feeling' territory. I noticed too as a cycled on, that I wasn't interested on what I could see or feel along the way, but I was only interested in arriving. Impatient to get to the next stage: the next hostel; the next stop. My frame of mind wasn't good at all as I approached the heavy gates of San Nicolau in Ponferrada and I hesitated. I anticipated an angry warden telling me there was no room for my bike and that I would need to go elsewhere, when to my surprise a young girl opened the gates with a smile. She pointed to a bike shelter to place my bike, and as I padlocked it and unbuckled my bags, she returned with a glass of freshly squeezed orange juice for me to drink. I was ecstatic. A smile, a place for my bike, and a glass of fresh orange juice and I was literally in heaven. A Scott Fitzgerald saying came to mind:

> "It was only a sunny smile, and little it cost in the giving, but like morning light it scattered the night and made the day worth living."

At another location along the way, an Englishman with a van ran a 'Mobile Repair Station' where he treated blisters with plasters and provided coffees, cold drinks, and a 'seat' for the pilgrims, spurring them on their journey. A good person, just giving of his time and energy, with nothing to gain but thanks from those in need. The pilgrimage makes you rely on strangers, and your inner resolve to endure. As I got nearer Galicia, the part of Spain that is Celtic and more like Ireland and Scotland, there were evenings outside hostels with music and banter and beers. These were fantastic nights where we shared our individual experiences, laughing at our weaknesses and outdoing each other with blisters and sprains but the determination to go on was universal. One of these evenings though ended abruptly with a French man, opening the window of his dormitory above us, and shouting that he was trying to get to sleep and could we all move on! He was angry, and I discovered as I crept into the dormitory, that I was sleeping in the bed right next to him. I was terrified that I'd awaken him.

There were some beautiful scenes of wheat fields, there were some magnificent descents into valleys with the wind blowing in my face and I had no need to pedal; there were some long monotonous stretches that were endless and then there were uphill struggles. It all seemed like a metaphor for life. I lost a favourite shirt too. I had handwashed it the previous evening and tied it to the back of my bike so that it would dry as I cycled. When I stopped at the next hostel it had 'gone with the wind' literally. I suppose like life itself, we are all gone, like the wind. That's what the Camino taught to me. I began to lose my attachment to things that a few days before had been so important. I was nearing the end of the journey. A reading I once found came to mind. It was called 'A Tandem Bike Ride with God', writer anon.

> *"I used to think of God as my observer, my judge, keeping track of the things I did wrong, so as to know whether I merited heaven or hell when I die. He was out there, sort of*

like a president. I recognised His picture when I saw it, but I didn't really know him.

But later on, when I met Jesus, it seemed as though life was rather like a bike, but it was a tandem bike, and I noticed that Jesus was in the back helping me pedal. I didn't know just when it was He suggested we change, but life has not been the same since I took the back-seat to Jesus, my Lord. He makes life exciting. When I had control, I thought I knew the way. It was rather boring, but predictable. It was the shortest distance between two points.

But when he took the lead, He knew delightful long cuts, up mountains, and through rocky places and at break-through speeds; it was all I could do to hang on! Even though it often looked like madness, He said, "Pedal!" I was worried and anxious and asked, "Where are you taking me?" He laughed and didn't answer and I started to learn to trust. I forgot my boring life and entered into adventure. And when I'd say "I'm scared!", He'd lean back and touch my hand.

He took me to people that had gifts that I needed, gifts of healing, acceptance and joy. They gave me their gifts to take on my journey, our journey, my Lord's and mine. And we were off again! He said, "Give the gifts away; they're extra baggage, too much weight." So I did, to the people we met, and I found in giving I received, and still our burden was light.

I did not trust Him, at first, in control of my life. I thought He'd wreck it, but He knows bike secrets, knows how to make it bend, take sharp corners, jump to clear high rocks, fly to shorten scary passages. And I am learning to shut up and pedal in the strangest places, and I'm beginning to enjoy the view. And the cool breeze on my face with my delightful constant companion, Jesus."

CHAPTER 20

Farewell my Faithful Steed

I was worried that arriving in Santiago, reaching my destination, would be an anti-climax, that it would be in some way disappointing. Physically, I was keen for the pilgrimage to end, but mentally I wasn't sure what to expect. When I arrived in Santiago, I headed straight for the Cathedral and surprisingly I needed to control my emotions at the Tomb of the Apostle, St James, who is reputedly buried there. Not only was it eerily calm and peaceful, it was also cool and clamour free. It was truly a place of rest after the heat and struggle of the journey. I felt as though I knew St James and that he had watched over and protected me throughout the pilgrimage. I felt it was like having a meeting with him at the end of the journey. It felt so special, and I stayed a while contemplating the mystery of it all. The Cathedral was empty, possibly because it was early, and whether St James is truly buried there or not, did not matter to me. The fact that thousands and thousands of pilgrims have made this journey over the centuries was very moving and I felt so fulfilled. I stayed for a while and prayed.

The next stop was the Pilgrim Centre where I received the document that proved I had undertaken the Pilgrimage. My *Compostelano* Certificate read that on

> *"22 mensis Juni ano 2003, Joseph Dillon concludes the pilgrimage of Nostri Hispaniarum Patroni ae Tutelaris Sante Jacobis."*

I left my bike at the Centre and headed into the Square where I had two delicious coffees and basked in the heat of the sun after my early morning start when it had been very cold. It was time then to head back to the Cathedral where I would concelebrate mass with other priests who had also completed the Pilgrimage.

The most striking feature of the Cathedral was the gigantic thurible or censer that burns incense during special services. I had heard about it, but only when seeing it did I realise just how impressive it was. At 1m 60cm high, and 80cm wide and weighing over 80 kilos when filled with grains and coals, it is an amazing vessel. It takes 8 people to manoeuvre it so that it swings in a pendulous, hypnotic motion. The aromatic scents that waft through the air have long been associated in sacred acts of worship from Egyptian and Roman times. It was believed fragrant scents pleased the Gods. However, in Medieval times in the Cathedral, burning incense was a way of purifying the air from the odour and germs brought in by pilgrims. As I watched the team pull the thurible to a certain height, and then skilfully control the enormous silver and brass orb as it oscillated at speed from one side of the sanctuary to the other, I was momentarily spell bound. The Cathedral by this time was filled with pilgrims, and as I distributed communion I was struck by the peaceful smiles on their faces. Their mission complete, an aura of well-being and deep gratitude suffused the air.

It was the Feast of Corpus Christi on the day I reached Santiago and there would be a procession through the town in the afternoon. I was interested to see in what way it would compare to the processions in Sao Paulo. The organisation was superb, and I noticed it was the same team of men who had swung the thurible who were now in charge of the procession which carried the Blessed Sacrament in a monstrance. It was on wheels and required a great deal of pushing and pulling to keep it going in the right direction. Many of the crowd who had gathered to watch, dipped their knees in deference as the Blessed Sacrament passed, while younger people in open air bars momentarily stopped chatting and drinking as a mark of embarrassed respect. The procession was dignified, and musicians played religious hymns throughout the route. However, altogether I noticed there were far less people in the procession than in those I'd seen in Sao Paulo.

I called my parish in Brazil and let them know my mission was complete. I had prayed for all my parishioners past and present along the way, and they said prayers of thanksgiving for me. As I made my way back to the hostel, I heard the Galician pipes playing. These reminded me of my roots, the Irish traditional music I loved so much and immediately I felt at home and uplifted at the same time. Reflecting on the churches I had visited from the beginning of my journey in Roncesvalles to Santiago, some had magnificent Romanesque architecture with curved stone arches, while other had intricate Gothic spires; some were queued with tourists, others were silent and empty. There were so many churches; some open; some closed; some welcoming; some cold. I suppose what I felt it lacked along the way was consistency. Perhaps a welcome pack in each church acknowledging that you are within Camino territory or perhaps background music playing in churches, so that when no one is there to physically welcome pilgrims, there is a presence, or an atmosphere, or a feeling of welcome? You know the feeling that a place is being prepared for you? It's a very comforting notion. Perhaps that's what I was looking for, and maybe twenty years later as I write, this has now happened.

The pilgrimage to Santiago deepens the relationship you have with yourself, but it is a very small part of life. It is all consuming and the outside world stops as you undertake it, but once completed, the certificate stamped, masses said, it is time to step back into the real world again where nothing very much has changed. It's the same old world out there with the same old problems waiting to be solved, and that for me meant saying farewell to my faithful steed – that is, my bike. As you'll remember it had been damaged on its way to Spain, and as I dismantled it, this time, to put in a bike bag to take by bus to Madrid, I was very careful with the gears and the brake pads. I would certainly recommend doing the Pilgrimage by bike, but only if you've completed a Bike Repair course, which of course I hadn't! This would have made things a lot easier, but then again, you live and learn along the way! I was all gung-ho at the start; a little more preparation wouldn't have gone amiss.

On the nine-hour bus journey to Madrid, flashbacks of the Pilgrimage entered my mind, and it became easier for me to see the beauty in each of the images. Perhaps God had been trying to say something to me, something I'd missed.

> *"For in Him were created all things in heaven and on earth, all that is visible and all that is invisible."* Colossians 1:16.

God's infinite presence had been evident throughout the Camino: in the forest animals, in the birds in the skies, in the tiny insects, in the fields of wildflowers and grain. By looking at these now through

God's lens, I could sense God's infinite love of our planet. A poem came to mind by Joseph Mary Plunket as the bus sped on its way. It is very well known in Ireland, as too is the author who was the highly educated intellectual leader of the Irish Uprising in 1916. He was executed by the British for the part he played in Ireland's fight for independence. His poem reflects on the beauty of all things created by God. It considers the need for us all to look beyond ourselves to find the true meaning of the universe. The poem is called "I See His Blood Upon the Rose."

"I see his blood upon the rose
And in the stars the glory of his eyes,
His body gleams amidst eternal snows,
His tears fall from the skies.

I see his face in every flower,
The thunder and the singing of the birds
Are but his voice-and carven by his power
Rocks are his written words.

All pathways by his feet are worn,
His strong heart stirs the ever-beating sea,
His crown of thorns is twined with every thorn,
His cross is every tree."

It reminds me too of the prayer attributed to St Patrick: "Christ Before Me". By putting Christ at the centre of your life, seeing through his eyes, walking in his footsteps, and suffering as he suffered, then you earn your crown, and of course the Kingdom of God. As I arrived in Madrid I felt Christ's presence, indeed my faith and connection with Christ had been renewed.

CHAPTER 21

Me and My Strange Ways

I returned to Brazil just in time for the two founders of SVD to be canonised: Arnaldo Janssen and José Freinademetz. Arnaldo Janssen was born in Goch in Germany and he established the Divine Word Missionaries in 1875 in Steyl in the Netherlands after the 'fallout' when Catholic priests were expelled from Germany during the Kulturkampf. He also founded two religious orders for women: Missionary Sister Servants of the Holy Spirit (SSpS) and the Holy Spirit Adoration Sisters (SSpSPA) also known as the Sisters of Perpetual Adoration. Arnaldo Janssen was canonised on the 5th October 2003 by Pope John Paul II.

Jose Freinademetz was born in the Tyrol in Austria and had a calling to serve as a missionary. He joined the SVD in 1878 and the following year he began his missionary work in Hong Kong and China. He never returned to Europe and died of typhus in 1908. He was canonised on the same day as Arnaldo Janssen. Almost 150 years later, the work of the Divine Word covers 79 countries with around 6000 missionaries. It is the largest Catholic missionary service in the world and is still rooted in Janssen's vision to make

Jesus' message known in every nation, to live and work in the most remote and neglected parts of the world, and to tell the stories of the gospel through a life of service and example. Our missionaries feed the hungry, care for the sick, shelter the homeless and promote spiritual formation and vocations. We provide healing, support and life-changing experiences through our love of Jesus and the love he shared with us. When I was in my teenage years, selling The Word magazine after mass in Dublin, I never envisaged the internet, the world wide web and social media. Neither would our founder Arnaldo Janssen – and it's great to see the Divine Word missionaries thriving in the 21st century. I often check out their website. https://www.svdmissions.org

The Jardim Miriam community was preparing to celebrate its 50 years, and the parish of Nossa Senhora Aparecida would at the same time be celebrating 35 years. A special anniversary book was prepared recording developments in the community over the years, especially the people who had contributed to making Jardim Miriam a safer and improved place to live. There were thanksgivings for everyone who had contributed to the parish. I had only served 16 years there, less than half of its lifetime, and when meeting priests and parishioners from previous years, it made me reflect on how transient life is. Parish priests come and go. As missionaries we come with our strange accents and strange ways, we share our vision of how we would like the parish to develop, we hope that it doesn't clash too much with the views of the parishioners and we really just want to see improvements, a strengthening of faith and a spreading of the Word. All the things I signed up to when becoming a Divine Word Missionary. I had developed my own niche in healing, not just physical ailments, but improving mental health too through herbal and floral remedies and therapies.

After 16 years in Nossa Senhora Aparecida, it was time for me to move on to become Parish Priest in Meia Lua, in Jacareí, 2 hours by car from Jardim Miriam in the church of Nossa Senhora Auxiliadeora. I would be starting over again with a new community, encouraging catechism groups for children, celebrating baptisms, weddings and funerals, as well as all the pastoral and liturgical work of a Parish Priest. I wanted to develop my herbal and floral treatments too as well as therapies, so I began clinics which we named Genesis. At the same time, I was also running courses in northern Brazil, in Rondônia and in Santarém, and every third Saturday, I went back to Jardim Miriam to help out in the clinic. I was doing too much, and at the age of 60 plus years, when the greatest part of my life's work was behind me, I found I was in greater demand than ever. I also found that I was up against the Charismatic Renewal Groups and coming from the Christian Based communities where spirituality is more social and political, I felt I was not quite the right person for this parish. I also had neglected my own health, and whether it was the change in diet, or whether I had been overdoing it, a cardiac problem arose, and I required a stent. After four years, I was relieved when the Bishop asked me to relinquish my post and let another Divine Missionary take over.

However, during the four years I spent at Nossa Senhora Auxiliadeora, I met so many wonderful people, especially in the CEBs (the Christian Based communities) that were well organised and proactive in promoting better health and social care. The CEBs also arranged for street masses to be said, sometimes in garages, sometimes in football fields. Wherever they could reach the people and these masses always had a joyful atmosphere. The council had provided the parish with a garden to grow its own medicinal plants and herbs. It meant that I was able to train the Genesis group in the manufacturing processes, and even although I left this parish in 2009, I was able to return frequently to give courses and the Genesis clinic is still going strong today, providing micro-doses and tinctures to communities all over Sao Paulo.

In Rondônia in northern Brazil, I was very impressed with the Caring for Carers courses where I was invited to speak. These were a mixture of creative workshops, Bach remedy training, and alternative therapies. In the evenings there were lighted processions, music and dancing. These were moving experiences and I felt such empathy with the suffering of all the carers whose burdens sometimes outweighed those they cared for. To this day, I thank God for carers and I pray for them each day. At another course in Rondônia I was introduced to Andrea. She was an Evangelical worker in the area interested in floral remedies. She asked us to undertake a course at the Agricultural Centre in Altamira. The people were extremely poor and lived a very basic life. They had known Sister Dorothy Stang, an American Notre Dame nun who had worked in this area, tirelessly campaigning for the rights of the poor to be free of the tyranny of the gangs of deforesters and drug-traffickers who forced them to surrender the land they had worked for centuries. She was gunned down in 2005. Shot in the abdomen four times and then in the back as she was on her way to a meeting of farmers trying to protect their land and livings. She had worked in the state of Pará in Altamira since 1966 and she was a true environmentalist and protector of the poor. She was known for wearing a t-shirt that said: "A morte da floresta – é o fim da nossa vida" – 'The Death of the Forest is the End of Our Lives.' A documentary was made about her life in 2009 and was narrated by Martin Sheen and directed by film maker Daniel Junge. It is called 'They Killed Sister Dorothy'. It is strange to think that in the same region of Northern Brazil today, things have become even worse for the indigenous people since Bolsonaro's presidency where loggers and deforesters have been given *carte-blanche* to destroy the rainforest. Only recently the British journalist, Dom Philips and the indigenous activist, Bruno Pereira, were murdered in the same vast and remote location in similar circumstances. They were trying to bring the horrific environmental story to the world's attention, but the gangs that operate in this area show no mercy to anyone who gets in their way of making a profit by corrupt and illegal means.

My final farewell in Jacareí was celebrated with a classical music open air concert beside the church, arranged by the depute mayor, Edvaldo Carneiro da Costa. The Jacareí Symphony Orchestra had never played in this setting before and in such a remote part of town. But they held us all spellbound with the sound of their strings and wind instruments. Normally it was ghetto-blasters playing a cacophony of funk music long into the night in this area. I thanked Edvaldo so much for organising such a thoughtful farewell concert. I wasn't at all surprised to hear that he was to become a theologian, and we are still in touch today.

I was leaving Jacareí as Parish Priest and was being sent to St Paul the Apostle at St Mateo's in Sao Paulo. But this wasn't farewell as I would continue to serve as a therapist to the community for many years, in the Genesis clinic that I helped to set up. I'm sure the

Bishop and the Charismatic Renewals were quite delighted to see the back of me and my strange ways.

CHAPTER 22

God's Presence

At the parish of St Paul the Apostle in St Mateus, I found that it was more difficult being an ordinary priest than being parish priest. Some people just don't think the same way and I often felt like Isaiah (55, 8-11): "my thoughts are not your thoughts". Over the years in this parish, I served several parish priests and I tried to build on my strengths, introducing herbal and floral remedy clinics, but even although the community was like Jardim Miriam and Jacareí, the clinics were never as popular. What I discovered was that classes in physical exercise were very fashionable. Lian Gong, which is a method of Chinese breathing, stretching and self-massage exercises was common, as too were circle dances as a way of easing tension. According to this tradition, simple circle walking or dancing is considered to strengthen the heart, mind and spirit and these classes were very popular. I began giving Lian Gong classes at 6.30am each morning followed by circle dancing. I also went back to Jacarei and Jardim Miriam each month to work in the health clinics, and as I no longer had the full responsibility of parish priest, I found this suited me perfectly. It was soon time for me to take a sabbatical in Europe and there was a course in our founder's city of Steyl in Holland that I had registered to attend.

The Divine Word house in Steyl is situated on the banks of the River Maas and my room overlooked the boats and barges as they passed by. It was so beautiful just to sit and watch them pass. The initial part of the course explored the historical background of the Divine Word. It was interesting to hear that following the French Revolution in 1789, when many bishops lost their land in France, they made their way north into Germany. However, a century later, Otto Van Bismark, Chancellor of the German Empire, spear-headed an anti-clerical movement in Europe, and that was the context for our founder, Arnaldo Janssen, to start a group of missionaries, to go forth and spread the Word across the world. The irony is, that perhaps now, Europe is in more need of missionaries to spread the Word than ever before.

This made me reflect on how or where our dreams come from? What factors motivate us to make our mark in the world? To give it meaning? Is it God speaking through us? The bible tells us that God spoke through his people. He spoke through the prophets, through Mary Magdalen, who spread the word of the Resurrection. He spoke through the gospels that told us of the One who was born, became flesh, and dwelt amongst us. That's why I'm here as a Divine Word missionary. I'm not worth much, but I'm still standing.

On the first day in Steyl we were asked to put ourselves before the Lord and reflect on our Life and our Mission. We were asked to answer questions on various aspects of our lives. Here are some of my reflections:

1. **People**: In the different parishes where I worked, I met people who were very important to my growth and formation.
2. **Events**: So many things over 40 years that I don't have time to analyse. But I remember Guaviruva a village on the banks of the Ribeira de Iguape river in the Amazon. I remember travelling with my van, travelling with youth to meetings in Registro and all the river communities. My parish of Francisco Xavier, the theatre groups, the passion plays on Good Friday, the one in the soccer field in St Marcos in the rain.....
3. **Churches**: The creative liturgies, full of meaning, expression of a living church. In St Marcos folk masses where everyone participated in singing. Masses by sister Miriam Kolling, hymns with liturgical and biblical content, hymns written by Cecila Domezi. Many of these hymns unfortunately have disappeared from the communities

today as they are no longer fashionable. But even popular music comes in and out of fashion. The church communities I served as the River Priest in Santarém. The companionship and camaraderie of the Processions, the Biblical Marathons, The Passion Play and the intensity of emotions we felt before and after each event. The Taking Care of the Caregivers in Rondônia and the Beth Bruno Project in Santarem. The gift I received in 1992 when I discovered alternative remedies. The consultations in Jardim Miriam. The setting up of a sister church in Wetzlar in Germany; the organisation of the exchange of expertise between our churches. The formation of the catechists within each parish. The bible courses in Jardim Miriam.

4. **Joys:** Seeing people feeling good after treatments. Or after a profound or pleasant liturgy. Seeing the theatre performances we produced bringing joy to the actors and the audiences.
5. **Pains**: Through my own fault, the many things that were not done. The joys that turned to pain at the death of friends. I always remember the pain caused by kidney stones in the Amazon, where eventually I had an operation, which led me to alternative medicine and a vegetarian life.
6. **Struggles**: How good it was to fight for health clinics that became influential Health Council Groups in St Marcos.

Belonging to the CEBs with the Latin American theology, preferring to choose the cause for the poor. *Allowing your life path to become alive within you.*

7. **Way of Life**: I am full of life, despite some health problems: heart; heel; knee. Sometimes I feel tired and without courage, but soon I am animated again. I don't spend a lot of time in a depressed state. I thank God for that and I still feel that deep down God still has a lot for me to do. I like being a member of the Divine Word, so many of us from different countries and cultures. There is no single way of life; every priest is different, and it is valuable to be different. It is good that no demands are made on each priest to follow a certain pattern. I think that is what hindered me in Jacareí. I felt like an employee of the church, which limited my freedom.
8. **Prayer**: Here I am in deep, and at this point, I must go even deeper. In this retreat I hope to do much more. I have already put myself before God who loves me. I want to dedicate my life again to Him, who is in fact the Love of my Life, even though I haven't talked a long time with this beloved. I prepare each mass well, especially the readings. We have the "lectio divina" (the prayerful reading of the bible) and it helps each of us to go deeper into community prayer.

9. **Service**: In the liturgy, in my earlier days, I was full of enthusiasm in organising the hymns, but today, after Jacarei, I have lost my enthusiasm. Maybe current 'happy clappy' songs of praise of the charismatics are too sweet and heavenly for me, (*so heavenly that they are of no earthly use*).
10. **Health Ministry**: With the sick and the old or with people with emotional problems, I feel good. I choose what I'm doing. I like the work (service) that I do and I make people happy. I hope they don't feel threatened by my presence in their home or in their life.
11. **Relationships:** With the priests in my house, I get along really well, but when I was in Jacareí, it seems that it didn't work out. I was very good with the laity, but with the charismatics, there was no love lost. I only became friends with them when they weren't praying or singing!
12. **Relationships with Women**: There is no chronological order in this list of places that I have friendships with women: Rio; Sao Paulo; Santarém; Dublin; Germany; England; Austria. 85% of my parish communities are women. They come in all ages and without them the church wouldn't function. For 40 years I have met religious and lay people who I can trust as true friends. I wonder if the people I met were signs of God's presence for me. Seeing their dedication, I can only say that they were. Have I been God's

sign to them? Because most of the people I have met have been women, I hope that they have found in me too, signs of God's presence.

The next part of our course is going to be in Rome, in Nemi where I had been before in the 1980s. Here in Steyl, there are 27 participants, all of them are men (priests), apart from one religious sister who is a course leader and will not be coming with us to Rome. The last time I was in Rome, I reflect that the person I chose to guide me through the retreat was a religious sister from New Zealand. For me, at that time, I was in the hands of God. I will leave this interpretation open while I continue to analyse my relationship with all the women in my life!

CHAPTER 23

Nemi – Plus ça Change

I had visited Nemi in Italy in 1983 when I was celebrating 10 years as a priest. Now, 30 years later, I was on my way by coach from Steyl to Nemi reflecting on how I'd heard the news of Antonio Meroth's death, on how my mother had visited and was so energetic and alive then. As the coach travelled past the Dolomites, I had the urge to climb the mountains and was frustrated as a mere bus passenger gliding by.

We stopped at the birthplace of the co-founder of the Divine Word: Jose Freinademetz and I was overcome with sadness as I heard about his childhood and saying goodbye, aged 27, to his mother, never to see her again, before going to China as a missionary. His mission was to love the people he served and for them to love him. I reflected on all the love I shared with the people I served. The deeply religious feeling that has no physical manifestation, and I thanked God for this. Slowly on that coach journey, we left the mountains behind us and the hillsides became full of vineyards as I spotted Florence in the distance. We would soon be in Rome. It crossed my mind that if the only prayer we said was thank you every day, it would be enough.

It was so good to arrive in Nemi and I instantly remembered the lake and its Roman history, especially the floating palaces built by Emperor Caligula that were sunk when he was deposed for being cruel and extravagant. These ornate marble-decked ships were raised from the lake in 1929 and were exhibited in Nemi Museum, however they were destroyed during WW2 when the Americans attacked the town, forcing the occupying Germans to set fire to the museum with the ships inside.

Ad Gentes is the Divine Word International Centre that promotes courses on spiritual renewal, Biblical and pastoral programmes. It is open to other groups who want to hold their own workshops or retreats. It is located about 30km south-east of Rome overlooking Lake Nemi which is an original volcanic crater. Everywhere in Nemi you are reminded that all things must pass. This is how the glories of the world pass. *Sic transit Gloria Mundi.* I read up more on Caligula and discover that he became Emperor in the year 37AD following the death of his father Tiberius. The army were loyal to him, calling him affectionately 'Little (Soldier's) Boot' that originated in his father's campaign in Germania. It didn't take long for the young Caligula to show his authoritarian and inhumane leanings. With public spending out of control he pursued and ordered the execution of the richest Romans and many important figures and confiscated their property in order to pay for his court's festivities. He was obsessed with the power and religion of Egypt and he considered himself a God. He had statues of himself made and placed in several temples and he spread the Egyptian cult for the Goddess Isis. Caligula was one of the most callous and controversial Roman Emperors noted for his notorious orgies. It was said that to humiliate senators and other elites, Caligula bestowed the post of Roman Consul on his horse, Incitatus, to show his underlings that their work was meaningless, and his horse could do it better. Several conspiracies were plotted against him, and finally he was assassinated in Rome by the Praetorian Guards in AD41. Caligula had become Emperor aged 21 and died aged 28. It is considered that he suffered psychotic episodes as a result of his excessive alcohol intake or perhaps even lead poisoning. On his death, his uncle Claudius was declared Emperor.

Excursions into Rome were planned as part of the course, and we were free to take the bus or metro and explore on our own. I visited the less well-known Basilica which is the oldest church in the West dedicated to the Blessed Virgin. It is called Basilica Santa Maria Major and is considered major because it is the most important church in Rome dedicated to the Queen of Heaven. The Basilica, built on the pagan temple of Cybele, is the only Roman basilica that has preserved the core of its original structure intact, despite several additional building projects and damage sustained by the 1348 earthquake. In the 5th century, Pope Sixtus III (432-440) restored it and dedicated it to Our Lady, whose motherhood the Council of Ephesus (432) had just proclaimed.

From the Basilica I visited the almighty Coliseum and of course one's mind turns fully to the might of Rome, and the Emperor Nero whose colossal statue stood at the entrance. The Coliseum was built initially on three levels and could hold around 50,000. Later it was extended with an additional fourth floor and with a capacity of 90,000 people. In anger, the large statue of Nero was torn down when Rome fell, and in its place, an empty space.

So what had Nero done to deserve such aversion? He was the nephew of Claudius, in whose reign, the Coliseum was planned. When Claudius died, probably assassinated, Nero, then aged 17, was proclaimed Emperor without opposition. This was AD54. With an initially good government, under the guidance of his mother, and the advisers Seneca and Burrus, he became more interested in the arts, and particularly music, to the neglect of the Empire. He gradually became overcome with a madness and unleashed a series of murders, rejecting his mother's influence on him, and killed her in AD59, and also his wife in AD62.

He was accused of having caused the fire that destroyed Rome (AD64) under the pretext of which, he began his persecution of Christians. His cruelty and disrespect provoked opposition from the military and the aristocracy. Nero committed suicide in 68AD when the empire revolted against him, led by the next Emperor Galba, whom Nero had had sentenced to death. However, Emperor Galba didn't last long on the throne either as this was the beginning of the spread of revolts and dissatisfaction with leadership.

The Forum, which is not far from the Coliseum, was the civic, religious and social centre of Rome. Here the citizens were told the news, listened to speeches of mystics, politicians and philosophers, paid their taxes and shopped in the stores or porticoes. They could visit the temple or simply chat and socialise. The rectangular plan of the Forum was repeated throughout the Empire and it followed a Divine Plan. The place was entrusted to the protection of the Gods and sacred through the augurs (soothsayers) through the 'reading' of the viscera of an animal. Only then, depending on the readings did the planners decide to construct the forum or not. If the signs were adverse, another location was chosen, more auspicious to the Will of the Gods. In a strange way, things haven't changed much as in Catholic countries, public buildings destined for large public works, are always blessed in advance.

A few days later we were on a pilgrimage to the place where Saint Maria Goretti died in the district of Nettuno, south of Rome. Maria Goretti was born on the 16th October 1890 into a farming family. She died because of inflicted injuries during an attempted rape at only 12 years of age. The assailant, Alessandro Serenelli, who had been continually asking Maria for sexual favours, approached her as she was taking care of her little sister in the family home. He threatened her with a dagger almost a foot long. When she refused, as she had done on previous occasions, he stabbed her 14 times. She was taken to hospital and was operated on without anaesthesia, but the injuries were beyond the doctor's ability to save her. During surgery Maria regained consciousness and insisted that she preferred to stay awake. The surgeons were surprised that she was still alive and in the presence of the police chief, Maria told her mother that Serenelli had already tried to rape her twice. As she had been threatened with death, she didn't tell anyone. The next day, she forgave her attacker and said she would meet him in heaven. She died 20 hours after the attack looking at a beautiful painting of the Virgin Mary.

Maria is patron saint to all victims of rape and sexual abuse. More than a century later, we are still dealing with young women who are murdered while defending themselves against predatory male rapists. It is more than a criminal act; it is an affront to the dignity of humankind.

In the enlightened 21st century I wonder if we are any the wiser to rulers who at first seem popular, but who really simply want to expand and aggrandise their kingdoms, who inflict war and terror on ordinary citizens, and lone individuals who see vulnerability as an opportunity for assault, sexual gratification and power. Sometimes I feel the prayers I said at Nemi are needed more than ever.

CHAPTER 24

Hungry For The Sun

The course in Nemi was made up of Indian and Indonesian priests and I seemed to be the sole European, who always wanted to sit in the sunshine and bask in its warmth. I am the eternal Irishman always hungry for the sun, so Italy in September was a tonic for me. The southeast Asian priests always sought the shade. The priest leading the course, spoke English with a strong Indian accent that I found difficult to understand, but all the other priests understood him perfectly, but had difficulty understanding me. Sometimes I felt so isolated and I longed to chat to someone in Portuguese. We spent a day on Anzio Beach and as the others gathered in the shade, I reached for a deckchair right under the sun. I felt the cultural difference acutely. Again, when we visited the Catacombs in Rome, which for me was such a claustrophobic and eerie place that I longed to exit, the group of priests clicked their cameras and chatted merrily throughout. The same thing happened when we visited the hermit's cave at Subiaco where St Bento began his life as a hermit in a cave. Subiaco is an Italian town in the Province of Rome in Lazio, 40km from Tivoli and beside the Aniene River. It is known for being a religious and tourist resort for its sacred grotto (Sacro Speco) in San

Benedetti. It is also famous as the first city in Italy where books were printed in the 15th century. The Latin name Sublaquem Subiaco (below the lakes) refers to the fact that the city was located beneath three artificial lakes created in the century 1AD by Emperor Nero. I felt this sacred cave deserved silence but with a bunch of priests armed with cameras, taking pictures and posing with the statue of the holy hermit, I looked for a place of calm in the garden, only to discover that it was also invaded by priests with cameras.

On another day's excursion, I went as a translator for a group that would visit an organisation called St Egidio that worked with all kinds of disaffected people and in particular, young drug addicts, who came to the centre to paint pictures and to be of company to elderly ladies. It seemed that this combination worked well for both young and old. Some of the young people are now bringing the old ladies to mass and taking them back home. The young ones do not attend mass, but they feel they are doing something valuable in accompanying the elderly there and back. We had lunch with the group of lay people, and it was very beautiful. We passed the SVD college in Rome on the way home, and while waiting for the bus, I went to look in the garden. There were so many plants that I started to pick aloe, persimmon, rosemary leaves, lemon leaves that I knew I could use in the presentation I was scheduled to make later in the week to the Asian priests about my parish and pastoral practices in Sao Paulo.

My presentation went well and I spoke about Brazil and the class seemed to like it. I prepared a mass to celebrate the feast of Our Lady of Aparecida and a team, that included my old friend Mick MacGuinness who had been with me in my first years in Brazil and who was now working in Nemi, helped me to arrange the altar that featured a Brazilian flag, a candle and a bible procession from the back of the church. Mick also had Tucum rings for everyone, a poignant symbol, that Europeans no longer 'take' from the indigenous people of Latin America, but they give. After the mass, we celebrated with a party and a little bit of the old Irish liquor. And as if by magic, the cultural barrier I was feeling so acutely, disappeared. The Indian priests praised me so much. The short poems I had read to them, the prayers, the small jokes. They came shaking my hands and saying wonderful things to me. Their simplicity was beautiful.

While in Nemi I also wanted to head to the mountains and climb as I had done thirty years before. I had been in Nemi when I had heard about Antonio Meroth's and Sister Angela's deaths. I wanted to visit Mount Lupone where I had held the mass in their memory. Mick MacGuinness dropped me off at 7am at the start of the ascent.

After two hours walking, I arrived at the summit that I thought was the place where I had celebrated mass. I remembered Antonio and Sister Angela and all those who had been part of my life over the years. I shed tears as I remembered those who had passed away and I also prayed for the people I had offended along the way too. But most of all I gave thanks for all the graces I had received. I drank some coffee and walked again towards another mountain that was a little higher, and as the sun shone on my face, it felt so good. I soon recognised however that the higher mountain was Lupone and not the lower summit that I'd prayed on. I stopped for a while to pray and came back satisfied that I had reached the point that marked a strong experience with God in my life.

The descent was hard on my knees, but they had taken me up to the mountains and I hoped they would be able to take me on other challenges. I always carried my 'bergstocks', the aluminium sticks that were already well worth the price I had paid for them several years before. The round trip was 17km and I returned to the village where the bus was scheduled to leave at 4pm but it had been cancelled and the next one wasn't due till 6.15pm. So I hitched a lift to Velletri (thanks to Baldo who stopped and picked me up), and from there I got a bus to Genzano where Mick picked me up and before I knew it, I was back at Ad Gentes in Nemi just in time for dinner.

It was important for us also to visit St Peter's Basilica and to receive a blessing from the newly appointed Pope Francis. The original St Peter's is situated on the site where Emperor Constantine in 324 – 349AD chose to honour St Peter, the first apostle with a small church. The greater basilica is situated where the Circus of Nero existed and had its first stone laid in 1506. Initially designed by Donato Bramante, the basilica would be built in the shape of a Greek cross, but after his death in 1514, the design would be modified.

Today it was busy and the rain was falling heavily but I was prepared with my plastic poncho and only my sneakers got wet. After the blessing, where I saw Pope Francis very well from St Peter's Square, we headed to the Tres Fontana Abbey, the place where St Paul was decapitated on June 29 67AD. His head was placed on a column and at the time of his martyrdom, it fell and bounced three times. At the site of each fall, a fountain opened up. In pagan times, this was a swamp area where Emperors who wanted Christians 'to disappear' were sent. Paul's execution is now the site of a Benedictine Abbey that was constructed in the Middle Ages. The remains of St Paul continue to be venerated and the altar in the Abbey has been built over the original three water springs. (Abbey Tres Fontes). Today as

I prayed in this huge church, my prayer was tiny in comparison to the size of the Abbey and the noise of the tourists.

I longed to return to the mountains and forest trails that surrounded Nemi. As they say, after drinking good wine, it's hard to be satisfied with less, so as soon as I could, I went walking again and found myself in Nemi's cemetery which was one of my favourite walks. I was sitting in the sun on the tomb of one O'Doherty/Bellacci. The first name was Irish, and the cross over the tomb was Celtic. I stopped there because it was warm in the sunshine and was a place to sit. I don't think O'Doherty was worried because I prayed for him. 'We're all going to end up like this,' I thought. 'Everyone. We must be prepared to meet God.' However, I could see that at the age of 70, I needed at least another 200 years in preparation. I hoped that when the day came, I'd be in good shape. There, surrounded by the dead in tombs, I was in no hurry to join them. All I could do was to pray for all those making that passage to eternal life: those in hospital; the elderly; the sick. 'Lord, give them strength to overcome the pain and when it becomes too much, let them slip into the deep sleep of eternal life.' I prayed.

It was so pleasant and warm in the cemetery, I had the urge to lie down, but I didn't want to frighten anyone who came in. Perhaps it was siesta time, and I could get away with stretching out? Perhaps I should listen to my inner voice and pray that I stayed a down-to-earth-priest, a bit like Pope Francis, who talks to everyone with love and affection. Things will change in the church, but the need for love and affection remains. But at that moment, I had been too long amongst the dead. It was time to return to class.

Fr Arlindo was speaking about his work amongst the homeless. He had organised our visit to St Edigio and I felt a connection with him and his work. It was nearly the end of September and I was feeling more at home now with the fellow priests. It would soon be my friend and colleague, Mick's 65th birthday, and I had to prepare a speech. This is what I wrote:

"*Miguel, I have known you for a long time. You were my provincial in Sao Paulo three times, but before coming to Brazil, we were together at Donamon Castle at our seminary at Roscommon (where a document was recently produced by the SVD that stated that Europe was currently a continent that needed missionaries.)*

Back then in 1966, we went to the seminary armed with two lethal weapons: the bible and the newly published Vatican II documents. We were children of a new age. Our teachers had a difficult time knowing what to do. They had all recently graduated from Techney in the USA and were totally unprepared for this type of seminarian. Mick was soon elected as class leader and representative and he needed to explain to the bishops why we went on strike against the poorly presented theology classes, that did not reflect what was in the Vatican II documents.

We were ordained together on December 17th in 1972. I came to Brazil on Oct 12th 1973 and Mick in January 1974. Then we went together to Rio de Janeiro to learn Portuguese and during the Carnival we walked and danced in the streets. Mick left Brazil for a job in the Generalate in Italy, but soon returned to Brazil. But not long after he was asked to become Dean of Ad Gentes here in Nemi. Mick cannot stand still, and as well as this post, he has become chaplain of the local hospital and helps all the priests in the local parishes. He speaks Italian very well. Congratulations Miguel. Happy Birthday on this day. We wish you a very happy birthday."

CHAPTER 25

St Francis of Assisi

October is the month that celebrates the feast day of St Francis of Assisi and it goes without saying, that we had a day's visit arranged to Assisi to see for ourselves the legacy of his life. The newly appointed Pope called himself after St Francis because: "he is the man of poverty; the man of peace; and the man who loves and protects creation." Never has St Francis' life been so relevant to the modern age and the issues our planet faces. He is patron saint of ecology and while I am not going to retell his well-known story here, instead I will take you through the churches in Assisi that we visited, each one situated in a significant moment of St Francis' life.

We set off at 5.45am by bus and the first church was Santa Maria dos Anjos (St Mary of the Angels), built between 1569 and 1679, based on the original 9th century church. The Porciuncula is a small church located within the larger basilica and is situated about 4km from Assisi in Umbria. It is the place where the Franciscan movement began. It was here that the young Francis, the son of a wealthy fabric merchant and the French Lady Pica from Provence, understood his true vocation and renounced the world of materialism to give his life in service of the poor.

The next point of reference was to pass the Porta de San Francesco which is the medieval gateway into the walled city of Assisi. The Papal Basilica of St Francis of Assisi lies within the great walls and is one of the most important places of Christian pilgrimage in Italy. With its accompanying friary, it is a distinctive landmark for visitors and has been a UNESCO World Heritage Site since 2000. It was the ancient site of criminal executions, and this is where St Francis wanted to be buried. The basilica, which began construction 1228 is built on the side of a hill and consists of two churches: an upper and a lower. St Francis' remains are buried in a stone tomb in the crypt. The interior of the upper church is an important early example of Gothic style in Italy. The upper and lower churches are decorated with frescoes by numerous medieval painters from Roman and Tuscan schools. The variety and quality of their work gives the basilica a unique importance in the development of Italian art of this period.

Our next task was lunch and just as Saint Francis had fed the birds, we did the same with our snacks, each of us wanting to attract more birds than the other. It depended on how hungry you were. We formed small groups and walked around the city, which was so beautiful and stopped at places that we thought were worthwhile, even the souvenir shops.

The Temple of Minerva (goddess of wisdom) was our next stop, which as the name suggests, is an ancient Roman building that now houses the Santa Maria of Minerva, built in 1539 and renovated in the Baroque style in the 17th century. The original temple was built in the 1st century BC at the request of Geus and Tito Caesius Prisco, who were two of the city's distinguished magistrates. The acknowledgement of the goddess Minerva derives from a female statue being found on the site, although they also found a statue of Hercules and it is considered that the original temple was in his name. From the original temple, 6 Corinthian columns are preserved in today's building, and it was from these columns that we entered the church. So steeped in Roman culture and mysticism is the exterior, I found it hard to see a statue of the Immaculate Conception in the interior. It seemed so out of place. I felt the best part of this temple were the original columns.

We continued on our way because we wanted to see the square in front of the Cathedral of St Rufino which is of Romanesque origin and built in the 5th century. This is the site where Francis is believed to have shed his material wealth: his horse, his knight's armour, his refined clothes, in favour of a life of poverty. It is in this church that

St Francis, St Clare, and many of his original disciples were baptised. The original baptismal font is intact. It was on hearing St Francis preach in this church in 1209 that St Clare was deeply touched by his message and realised her vocation to work with him in service of the poor. We wanted to visit the church dedicated to St Clare so we walked even further, still with energy for more, until we found the Basilica of Santa Chiara. She founded a monastic religious order for women in the Franciscan tradition and wrote the Rule of Life. These are the first monastic rules to be known to have been written by a woman. She worked alongside St Francis and cared for him up until his death in 1226. She then continued to promote his work and the growth of her order, writing letters to abbesses all over Europe and frustrating every attempt by each successive pope to impose a rule on her order that would dilute the radical commitment to corporate poverty. She did this despite health problems, until her death in 1253. After her death, the order she founded was renamed and referred to as the Poor Clare's. About 600 years later in 1872, the remains of St Clare were transferred to a newly built sanctuary in the crypt of this church where it can still be seen today.

But of course, we all wanted to visit St Damien's church, the place where it all started. This is where St Francis and his followers built their own church with an outdoor garden area for growing vegetables and for feeding the poor. He and his disciples were never too proud to beg from others to feed and share food with the lame, the dispossessed and the homeless. Soon the work of St Damien's became an inspiration to other communities, and it is here where many of the legendary stories of St Francis took place. Eg: kissing the leper, taming the wolf and receiving the stigmata.

We went through the Porta Nuova and walked down about a kilometre to the church of St Damien's that was so beautiful that you really felt the presence of God. Perhaps this was because there were notices for silence and no photographs. Even our noisy priests respected the atmosphere of this unique place.

St Francis rejected fame and fortune that would have come to him as a glorified knight after fighting wars against Perugia and beyond. During his first experience of being a soldier in battle he was imprisoned for almost a year, and despite his reputation for singing songs and keeping the spirits of all his fellow prisoners up, it was this experience of being in the chains, that convinced him of the senselessness of war. On his release, he and his compatriots were welcomed home to Assisi to a huge celebration, but soon he learned that he would need to fight again, as his father began to equip him with a new horse, a suit of armour and briefings on his next battles. This is when St Francis made up his mind to reject all that war stood for. He wanted to live a peaceful life, helping those who suffered, often because of war. He sold all his wealthy clothes and goods to buy construction materials to build St Damien's, and to feed his fellow construction workers, many of whom had been imprisoned with him previously. These actions triggered the ire of St Francis's father, who disowned him and at the age of 22, St Francis accepted his father's decision to disinherit him, and he renounced all his father's assets.

Pope Francis asked: What is the peace that St Francis received, experienced and lived and that passes on to us? It is the peace of Christ, born of the greatest love of all, the love of the cross. It is the peace that the risen Jesus entrusted to his disciples when he was in their midst. (John 20:19-20) Franciscan peace is not something sweet. This is not the real St Francis. Nor is it a kind of pantheistic harmony with the forces of the cosmos......this is not Franciscan either! It's not Franciscan, but the notion that some people have invented! The peace of St Francis is the peace of Christ and is found by those who 'take up' their 'yoke', that is Christ's command: Love one another as I have loved you. (John 13:34; 15:12) This yoke cannot be borne with arrogance, presumption or pride, but only with meekness and lowliness of heart.

Pope Francis has tremendous faith, and his strength comes from his personal contact with Christ. “It is not I who live, it’s Christ who lives in me”.

We were all ready to go home by the time we arrived at the bus parking space. We left at 5pm, and it took 3 hours to get back to Nemi. We were back just in time for dinner at 8pm.

CHAPTER 26

Forest Trails

The forest trails around the hills of Nemi were a course in nature itself. As often as I could, on free days, I would walk through these trails discovering something new each time. On this particular walk, it had rained a lot the day before and leaves that had fallen from the trees were glistening on the track. Everything was so alive after the rain, and it felt as though each plant was saying:

"Look at me! Amn't I perfect? Don't I radiate health? Take me with you, I can totally surrender to your medicines. I won't keep any of my active ingredients away from you. I will surrender them all. I am good for colds and flus. I am also good for anti-this and anti-that....." Now if a mere plant can do that? Why can't I, a human being, do the same thing? Submit myself totally?

When the trail ended, I had two options: to go to Albano, or Castel Gandolfo. I chose Gandolfo, but as the trail slowly became an asphalt road with traffic on it, it wasn't half as magical. Castel Gandolfo is a town located 24 kilometres south-east of Rome in the Lazio region of Italy. Occupying a site in the Alban hills, overlooking Lake Albano, it has a population of nearly 9000 inhabitants and is considered to be one of the most beautiful towns in Italy. Within the town the Apostolic Palace of Castel Gandolfo lies, and it is the summer residence for popes now and in days gone by. Although the palace is situated within the borders of the town, it has extraterritorial status as one of the properties of the Holy See. During World War II, an unknown number of Jewish refugees took shelter in the palace under the guard of the Vatican City. Pope Pius XII died in the palace in 1958, as did Pope Paul VI two decades later in 1978. Pope John Paul II had a swimming pool installed which was criticized by the paparazzi who took photos of him there. Pope Benedict XVI flew to the palace at the conclusion of his pontificate on February 28, 2013. In March 2013, Pope Francis visited Pope Benedict at the palace for lunch.

I had brought lunch with me and stopped on the way to read and rest my bones. In fact, the old bones were doing fine that day, the main difficulty was my feet, but that was mainly caused by walking on the hard asphalt surface. Now I needed to make a decision, to go down to the lake and find a trail that would take me to the point where I started or to go by road? Well, I went on the road. The traffic was heavy and the road was narrow. It took me around an old Convent named Santa Maria ad Nives di Palazzo. (Madonna of the Snow). This was a Catholic place of worship located in the municipality of Rocca di Papa in Frascatti. Next to the church was the former convent that originated in the 11th Century. It was in a picturesque location overlooking Lake Albano, and it reached its height in the mid-18th century after a series of renovations overseen by cardinals that featured hanging gardens and a magnificent reception hall for visiting guests. However, various closures and occupations later, the convent fell into disrepair, but since the 1920s it has become a summer retreat for English seminarians and it is well maintained.

When I finally arrived at the convent, my feet were aching from the road walk, and I was so pleased to return to the forest trail where I was immediately protected from the hot sun by the canopy of trees. How do I express my feelings on these hikes and especially walking through the forest? On the winding trails it is difficult to keep your direction. If it wasn't for the sun, I would be lost completely. I say to myself, "I must go the way the sun tells me. The direction that will take me home".

Autumn was starting to show itself, the leaves were falling and the noise that is made when I passed in the forest became something mystical, there was a special "shuu shuu" sound when I passed in the fallen leaves. It was a special sound and it felt very pleasing to my ears. This year I have been blessed with walking through woods and forests. Normally I like to go out in the open or on the top of hills or mountains, but what I have been achieving only a short distance from the house in Nemi is as much as I ever could have achieved on the mountains.

The nuts and flowers are everywhere on the ground. The sweet chestnuts, which are clustered in trios inside their brown mossy shells are edible, unlike their close relatives, the horse chestnut, with their spiky green shells and clear, polished, brown nuts that are poisonous. The flower of the sweet chestnut tree: the Castanea Sativa is one of Bach's Flower remedies. It is one of the last flower remedies Bach discovered before he died at the age of 50 in 1936. He wrote this:

"Sometimes one has to be aware of feeling extremely helpless and unable to ask for help, or at the mercy of circumstances, like a new-born baby, a feeling of being in the middle of nowhere, with no past and no future, and in a current state of despair." He was explaining the need for trust. This thought made me feel that I needed to learn how to trust the Lord more. How to give myself into His hands. I needed to trust His goodness and grace. It is my mission to denounce injustice, violence, repression, selfishness and fear. But when and how? I sometimes feel that I still don't trust God enough to leave everything in His hands. While I'm waiting for His answer, I go ahead and do things my own way. Maybe that's why I walk alone? Or maybe I don't always feel the need for company?

It was soon time for me to return to Brazil, renewed in all that I had learned from my courses in Steyl and Nemi. I still felt there was a lot for me to do in Brazil despite my 70 years of age. I felt strongly that I wanted to embed the work that I had begun with the sick and in improving the health and spirit of others who live in impoverished situations. I hoped that when I returned to Sao Paulo that I would not be transferred from this work, but if I was, I would have the ability to obey. I had been given the opportunity to pray here especially on the forest trails. To go to my inner self and to give God time, so that I could be imbued with the joy of being a missionary. It's strange, but I found I could not separate my time on inner prayer from my time spent on the trails and mountains. This was where I found that I was truly contemplative, and I returned spiritually refreshed despite my aching knees and feet. It is perhaps the details that I observe when walking that make me so mindful of God; the shapes, the colours, the hardness, the softness, the smells, the cold, the heat, the sun, the shadow, the lightening; the thunder.

I think what pleased me most during this sabbatical, was when I was in Steyl, some course members took unwell with stomach upsets and I was able to collect and administer some herbal remedies from the banks of the River Maas, where I had found a laboratory of nature's blessings in the form of plants on the wayside. My eyes were opened to these wonders once again, as they had been in 1992, when I first discovered their potency. My mission then was renewed, to heal the injured body. Not just the physical, but the holistic body, the spirit and the soul. And I wanted to continue this practice through medicinal plants, herbs and flowers.

I learned a new German word in Steyl: *gastfreundshaft* which means to be hospitable; to accept someone just as he or she is. Each meeting, no matter how long or short, is an opportunity to find grace in that other person. To see God present in that person. No matter whether a body is beautiful, ugly, aged, broken, wounded, tortured, sick, mistreated, humiliated, my mission is to see beyond the outward, and seek the inner God within. To accept each person, just as he or she is. It was beneficial to explore so deeply the roots and traditions of the Divine Word Mission and to see how it has developed over the years. It was wonderful to be within the group of international priests who spoke so many different languages, whether from Indonesia, India, Vietnam, Ghana, Philippines, Poland, or Portugal. And definitely the greatest challenge I found was in that word 'obedience'. I knew I had challenged my bishops in the past in Sao Paulo and had not always been happy to do their will. I suppose this is a key phrase I will take away with me in understanding Jesus' mission. *It is not my will, but Yours.*

The organisation of both courses was outstanding. The instructions, the tours, the pilgrimages, the material for reading, the diaries, the content of the lectures and the reflection on our relationships, especially with women. Maybe role play would have been a better way to confront how it feels to be a woman surrounded or being led by macho priests. It is perhaps only by taking on each other's roles that we can see more clearly the prejudices and injustices from another perspective.

My final evaluation before saying goodbye to Nemi was that the staff were wonderful and sincere; the guest rooms were comfortable, and the food was delicious. Best of all, the water pressure in the showers was simply amazing. I am prepared now to return to the world, where everything I have learned will be put to the test.

CHAPTER 27

Roots

Before heading back to Brazil, I had to stop off in Ireland, to visit the family. I am not very good at packing and cleaning. I always leave things until the last minute and it's at times like these I wish I had a personal assistant. Fr Peter took me to Ciampano Airport and my sister Julie was waiting for me at Dublin Airport. Soon I was with my brothers and sisters, attending masses, eating pub lunches and wearing warm and very welcome woolly jumpers. From Dublin, I went to the SVD house in Maynooth and then to Donamon Castle, in Roscommon where I began my life as a seminarian in 1966. I was different back then: pleasant, humble, and well-behaved. Now I'm trying to recover some of that goodness but I can't go back. I must build on the 'ruins'. I learned that in Rome. What was once a pagan temple, became a Christian church. At least I learned the merits of reconstruction in Rome.

The weather was 7–11 degrees in Roscommon. The sky was grey and they said that Thursday and Friday would be even colder!!! Heavens, it was time for me to pack my things and say goodbye to Ireland. I hoped that Sao Palo would be 27 degrees or more.

Meanwhile, I celebrated mass with the priests who lived in Donamon Castle. My room was at the very top and there were so many stairs to climb. I questioned why I was there, but I wanted to keep in touch with the remaining priests. I noticed however that the only thing that seemed to be growing in the SVD in Ireland was the number of priests now buried in the cemetery. When I joined in 1966, there were only two graves, but here there were more than 30. One of the surviving priests was 92 and he rode around everywhere on his bicycle. The others were very frail. It would be old age that would take them in the end. I thought the only reason I'm still standing is because God wants me to do more, to pay for my past sins. So perhaps I may need to live another 30 years!

As well as missing Brazil and preparing for my return, I was beginning to become quite anxious that I would be unable to live up to the expectations that people may have created of me during my absence. I am still Joe, but the people who received emails from me in Sao Paulo may not be used to hearing my deep searching and expressions of faith. Yes, they hear my sermons in church, they know that I'm not keen on the charismatic movement and expressing my inner thoughts. Maybe they would become more demanding of me – not simply wanting to hear my words, but wishing me to bare my soul?

Returning to my sister Julie in Malahide on the coast of County Dublin, I walked around the grounds of Malahide Castle and admired the village, the beach and all its attractions. I visited my two old friends Noel and Dick, who were both looking after their ailing wives. Noel, whose wife Jean had had a stroke, and Dick whose wife was suffering from Multiple Sclerosis. I admired them both for their devotion and service. My departure day came round so quickly and at the last minute I needed to pack in a hurry in order to catch an earlier plane to London for my connection to Sao Paulo. I reached Sao Paulo and I was met by my team of Bach Floral remedy therapists who were celebrating the completion of their course. I joined in with them. It was as if I'd never left.

However, I will return to Ireland twice more in the coming decade and be with my family, singing together with my eldest brother John playing the guitar. He is a songwriter and ballad singer. I find it's such a great feeling singing together. Music, hymns, songs and melodies awaken the memories of the 'good old days.' It's also fascinating to see the next generation thrive. I can see how important the structure of the family is, especially as I dip in and out every 5 years. My roots: my nieces and nephews; great nieces, great nephews, making their own lives, seeking happiness and fulfilment. I can see that families coming together for celebrations is so important; it helps us all to become good human beings, passing on our love and values to each generation. My sister Mary is an accomplished artist in Carlow and my brother-in-law Cecil is a writer and his wife Julie is a golfer, a gardener, and an amazing hostess. They are all so talented each in their own way. My brother Vincent has had a heart operation but continues to work in his plant and herbal nursery business and Mary has had an operation but still manages to bake the best apple pies for me to share with the priests wherever I am staying in the SVD communities. As well as being talented, my family are a persistent and stubborn bunch!

On one of my visits to Dublin, I visited Kilmainham Jail, the place where the Irish freedom fighters faced a firing squad and where the cruelty and brutality of the British government will forever be remembered. It's more than 100 years since this happened, and I couldn't help but feel the immense optimism of an independent Ireland within Europe. I also visited the exhibition at the GPO in central Dublin, the location of the Easter Rising where the men and women initially rebelled against the British authorities, and although this bid ended in failure, it led to Irish Independence and the creation of the new state. The architecture of the GPO occupies a place of symbolic significance to the Irish. As does James Joyce, an Irish novelist, short-story writer and poet. Born in Dublin in 1882, he contributed to the modernist avant-garde movement and is considered to be one of the most influential and important authors of the 20th century. Shortly after the publication of 'Ulysses' he said,

"For me I always write about Dublin, because if I can reach the heart of Dublin, I can reach the heart of every city in the world." In the particular, the universal is contained. He lived most of his life outside Ireland and died in Zurich in 1941.

So from thousands of miles away in Sao Paulo, what do I feel about the city of my birth? Do I feel some special relationship with the city itself? I would have to say no. But I think that a city is not simply the buildings, but it's the people who live there. For myself I have spent more of my life outside Dublin than in it. I left Ireland at the age of 30, and the people I am closest to, are my friends in Brazil. But I have always believed in continuity and having roots. I always say '*you can take a man out of the bog, but you can't take the bog out of the man*'. I cannot reject Ireland. It's where my family and friends live and it continues to be part of my history. When I see the 'grandchildren' - the great nieces and nephews, I see how the story continues. I see how time goes by and that they soon will be making life-decisions of their own. May God give them grace wherever they may be, to be happy and fulfilled. But in the meantime, I call Brazil my home and my *raison d'etre*.

CHAPTER 28

Accidents Happen

In Sao Paulo I was happy to continue with the pastoral care in the community, visiting the sick and supporting the carers. I would continue with my health clinics as well as celebrating mass and doing baptisms and marriages. But I would no longer be responsible for the day to day running of a parish. At St Paul the Apostle, where I was an assistant priest, we awaited the arrival of a new parish priest who had been appointed. He was originally from India but he had worked in the state of Rondônia and he was in his early thirties. While I had been away in Europe, a caretaker priest had come to keep things going in the parish, but I could see that there was much work to be done to keep the catechist and liturgical groups going as well as the pastoral care of the youth groups.

Slowly we began to see the changes the new parish priest would implement. The charismatic movement was given prominence and their energetic singing, hand clapping and praying with arms outstretched began to take over in the traditional liturgical masses. The Politics and Faith group, which I had helped to set up, was forbidden. I was astonished at his actions, especially as in my forty plus years as a priest, and especially now with Pope Francis, whose theology of empowerment for the poor was so welcome, and yet this new parish priest, held the view that the CEB's had no relevance in our parish. At first, I attended the parish council meetings, but I soon found that I was contradicting him, and this was not pleasant. A new priest arrived and backed the parish priest, so I stopped going to the meetings and continued to support the parish in baptisms, marriages, burying the dead, and visiting the sick. I participated in all the celebrations and processions, as well as travelling to other parishes doing my health and alternative therapy clinics, in which the parish priest showed no interest.

And then I had an accident to my knee, which was already weak from a stretched tendon. This time, it required an operation called a *tenorrhaphy*. This resulted in physiotherapy and being told I could not put any weight on it for 6 weeks. The parish priest used this as an opportunity of 'freeing' me from the parish and I was sent to the Old SVD Priest's Home in St Amaro to recover. I had vowed, that as long as I was standing on two feet, I would never go to the Old Priest's Home, and I would keep on working at St Paul's. But herein lay the problem. I couldn't stand on my feet, and I needed to be in a wheelchair for 6 weeks. Without being consulted, it was considered "better that I should go to St Amaro to be looked after by people who could take better care of me."

While there were many people in the parish ready to look after me, including Nina de Conquista, a therapist who lived near the hospital, as well as other therapists, it was to no avail. After the operation, I was taken to our SVD Home called Jose Freinademetz to learn to walk again and let the power of God flow through me as I walked through this valley of tears.

Physiotherapy would start the following week and I felt so frustrated because I was no longer active and able to help others. During this time, I read a lot and finally had time to keep up with correspondence that I had neglected. I prayed the daily readings of the mass in English and Portuguese, and these gave me a basis for some religious and some not so religious reflections.

I discovered the English mystic Juliana of Norwich ($14^{th}/15^{th}$ century) who said that God didn't limit himself to 'sacred' places to reveal himself. One of the places where she discovered this was in the toilet, which in the 14th century was not the most hygienic place for God's revelations. If God can reveal himself in such conditions, then he cannot be excluded from anywhere under the sun. Following my reflection on the theology of toilets, I discovered a very simplified view of the human being. They are Trinitarian. They eat, urinate and defecate. If these functions are all working, there is joy. When any of these malfunctions, there is suffering and a wish to be restored. I said great prayers at this time to accept the discomfort and to be grateful for all that I was able to do.

I became acquainted with another theology based on Humility which Paul said in Philippians (Phil 2, 5-11) '*so that in the name of Jesus, every knee bends in heaven and earth*'. I needed to pray that I had a perfect recovery and who knows I would soon be able to bend my knees and give thanks to God. I'm sure my Bach remedies helped me accept the situation and keep me in a positive mood. The visitors that came were all my students from the Bach classes, who were by this time fully trained therapists treating people far and wide. They came from the parish of Nossa Senhora Aparecida where I had worked for 16 years. Another group came from my parish of St Paul's in three cars. The distance by bus from St Paul's to St Amaro can take 2 hours or more depending on the traffic. They brought picnic baskets and we ate heartily. They were from the Moses Liberator community where I taught Lian Gong classes and held bible groups. They informed me of the changes the parish priest had made since I had gone, and that the Faith and Politics group were now meeting privately in their homes as he had banned them. As well as feeling pain in my knee, I felt pain in my heart for this group, as I was one of the founding members. We had changed our name from Micah the prophet to JUPIC, which is a recognised group in the SVD and means: Justice, Peace and Integrity of Creation. Pope Francis was calling on us to be an 'outgoing' church, to go beyond the boundaries of the church doors, and work with those in pain and suffering. I had to speak out.

On my last visit to the hospital for a check-up, instead of returning to St Amaro, I decided to go back to the parish. The parish priest and his assistant were not happy to see me. They called the Provincial in charge, Joao Batista to come and see me. He denounced me publicly, and asked me why I had stopped communicating with the other priests and why I had not attended parish council meetings? Well, what could I say? I explained my position, that what was happening in our parish was against everything the church had ever taught. This happened just 5 weeks after my accident and my knee still hurt a lot, as did my mind.

I was given no alternative but to return to the Old Priest's Home and it was very difficult to explain in front of the other priests in the home why my 'confrères' ignored me. There was not even a message or a telephone call in all the time I was there asking how I was doing. This did not leave much room for conversation at the dinner table. I knew then that I had to leave the parish of St Paul's. As the Acts of the Apostles said: *They were "united in one body and one soul"* (4,32). Or "*they met constantly to hear the apostles teach and share common life to share bread and pray*". (2,42). We were certainly not living like this at St Paul's. My health and social empowerment groups were what inspired and sustained me, but for now I was without a voice and stability. I had to dig deep and reflect on my promises I had made when on sabbatical at Nemi. There I had been forced to examine my relationships with all those in my ministry and how I could improve on them; I had also identified my difficulty in being obedient – that I always preferred to do things 'my way' and I had promised myself to be more obedient, and humbler. Would I be able to return to the parish once my knee was fully healed, and keep my head down, and go along with the changes in a positive *mind over matter* way? Or would I stick to my principles and continue contradicting the parish priest in the hope that he would one day see the light and change his ways?

It was at this time that I really missed being able to take to the mountains. You need nothing more than your legs, a bottle of water, a good pair of boots and a jacket if it's going to be cold. Nature clears the mind. A walk in a natural environment has a huge positive impact on mental health. Walking in nature is more beneficial than in urban areas. I always felt relieved of worries when walking in the mountains. When I came home, I never felt tired, but invigorated. Now, with my knee strapped, and being unable to 'walk off' my problems, I felt frustrated, but my mind was activated as I remembered all the mountains I'd climbed. The mountains put things in perspective. As I rehabilitated, I recorded the mountains I'd climbed in my life:

1964 –	Norway, Galdhoppigen, 2469m
1965 –	Austria, Grossglockner, 3798m
1960 -66 –	Ireland, Carrauntoohill, 1039m; Ireland, Lugnaquilla, 925m
1978 –	Austria, Lamsenspitz, 2508m
1983 -	Italy, Lupone, 1378m
2013 –	Italy, Lupone, 1378m
1983 -	Switzerland, Mt Santis, 2502m
1990 –	Brazil, Agulhas Negras, 2791m
2005-2008 –	Austria, Rietzei Griesskogel 2880m; Reicenspitz, 3260m
2017 -	Ireland – Sliabh Donard, 850m

Now there was still one mountain that I longed to climb, the mountain of my dreams: the Matterhorn, 4478m. That would certainly clear my head....

CHAPTER 29

Letting Go

Once I had recuperated, I returned to St Paul the Apostle's, and kept my head down. Seven months after my accident, I was beginning to walk without assistance, and at last I could ride my bicycle. I was once again teaching on the diploma courses in Floral Remedies and Alternative Remedies in several parishes and as Christmas approached, I reminded myself to be humble, to be obedient and I also remembered that in Nemi I had pledged to begin to 'Let Go': to let go of my possessions, my wishes, my entire being in the end, like Christ, emptying himself of self, when he died on the cross, accepting, rather than fighting his fate.

For myself, this was my struggle - letting go: of my power, my knowledge and experience that I had built up over the years. At least now I was sharing this with the students so that my health projects could continue without me; but I had to keep reminding myself of not becoming too attached to people and to things; not to accumulate. I think that is what always fascinated me about Christmas; the mystery of the incarnation, and God becoming flesh, not in a palace surrounded by armies and guards, but as a child, born in poverty in a stable for animals.

But what does his birth signify? That something significant can come from the insignificant. King Herod and the religious leaders of the time could not see this, but the birth of Jesus has always reminded me, that by serving the weak, the unimportant, the elderly, the sick, the homeless, the losers, the unloved, something wonderful happens. By losing myself in them, it is as if, the glory of the Lord is revealed.

Reading Paul's text to the Philippians (2, 6-11) we see that Jesus emptied himself of 'self', so that we, 'by emptying ourselves, by removing even our own notion of God that we have accumulated through history, that only then, can we see his image in our '*poor*' brothers and sisters'. I learned that by emptying myself even of the sacred concepts I had constructed in my mind, I still had many prejudices. As an example of emptying myself of 'self', I looked to Julio Lancelotti, a Parish Priest in the Mooca area of Sao Paulo, who said, "I don't work with the homeless, I live with them." He believed in seeing the image of Christ, no matter the circumstances, in every human he encountered.

However, no matter how I tried, the politics of Brazil got me down. Under the right-wing presidency of Bolsonaro, not only had the rain forests suffered, but the Pastoral Bible I have always used when helping parishioners understand the daily/weekly readings, had been deemed a Marxist/communist tool by a priest and friend of Bolsonaro. This was because of the interpretations of the text in the footnotes. I took consolation by the fact that the Catholic church had always contained priests, bishops and a hierarchy who did not accept a Christ who cared for the poor, fed the hungry, visited the sick and the dying. If they did accept this Christ, then they would have needed to change their lives dramatically to fight for a more just and equal society.

Again, I needed to learn to let go of my strong feelings on this subject and try to accept them. The right-wing movement of Tradition, Family, Property (TFP) was growing in Brazil, and indeed other New Right movements were emerging globally, all founded in finely edited Christian ethics, concerned more about conserving power, knowledge and material wealth than sharing with others and 'letting go'. I too could select from the gospels and carefully edit sections of the bible that would be in direct conflict with the New Right's interpretation, but that would just be rising to the bait. It was better to accept and 'let go'. In order to detach myself from the politics I found it therapeutic to immerse myself in the herbal plants used in my health projects, some that have fascinated me since I was a boy growing up in Dublin. For example:

The **Plantain** (Plantago Major). It was the first herbal plant I studied and it grows everywhere in Brazil. It grew in Dublin too, and I remember my father struggling to dig it out of our lawn because he considered it a weed. In my studies, I discovered that it was not a weed, nor a pest, but a cure for diseases and pestilences. Amongst its many healing properties, it is known to cleanse the blood, and the tea from its leaves is a healing agent for gastrointestinal problems. The scalded and cooled leaves when applied to skin wounds such as ulcers, dog bites or burns, soothes and calms. The entire aerial part of the plant can be used including the leaves and the stalk and in Brazil it is known by several different names depending on the state: *tansagem*; *transagem*; *tanchagem ou sete nervos* and it is sold in quality health food shops.

The **Cabbage (Brassica)** plant. Again, so common in Ireland as I grew up as a staple meal: cabbage ham and potatoes, and yet its medicinal properties are endless. The leaves should be well washed and can be used as poultices for many skin disorders including eczema, dermatosis, pain and swelling relief of the breasts while breast-feeding, and soothing itchy skin. Cabbage juice is known to heal stomach ulcers and eaten daily some finely sliced raw brassica leaves with a teaspoon of olive over a 3–4 week period, is also a treatment for duodenal ulcers. Kale is also used for its medicinal properties, and like other brassicas, it should not be cooked, as this can destroy its high multi-vitamin content. Lightly tossed in olive oil is a common way of serving brassicas and this dish is considered to lessen the muscle pain of arthritis, rheumatism and gout.

Guaçatonga (Casearia Sylvestris) is a native plant of the Amazon and was used by indigenous Indians as an antidote for snake or insect bites. They had observed lizards eating the leaves after being bitten by a snake, and they also noticed that lizards would only face off a snake if they were in an environment where guaçatonga grew in abundance. In Brazil, this plant has various local names such as *cha de bugre*, *burgrinho* or *café do mato* (wild coffee plant) and *café brava*, of which the leaves and beans, when boiled and cooled, have a slight caffeine content and a natural appetite suppressant that is used as a slimming aid and also has anti cellulose properties. Using the leaves and bark only, it is an effective treatment against herpes, although it does not eliminate the virus. As a tea it promotes circulation, keeps cholesterol low, and cleanses the blood. The application of the tea as a compress soothes the skin of acne, pimples and bruises.

These plentiful plants that grow so easily in Brazil, contain some of nature's natural remedies. However, it is important for users to be aware of safe doses and treatments especially if they are pregnant or on other medication.

I had managed to 'let go' of all the issues that concerned me, when I heard by surprise that the parish priest was to be transferred to another parish, and an old friend, Norberto, who I had worked with at Nossa Senhora de Aparecida, would be taking over until a new one was appointed. Norberto and I had got on so well and I was happy to see him again. I remembered fondly our pizza nights and the visits from his father from Germany. It was wonderful to see him, and I knew once again the parish of St Paul of the Apostle was in safe hands. Within a few months, a new parish priest, Father Bonifacio was appointed, and Norberto was nominated as Bishop of Ji Parana in the state of Rondônia. Father Bonifacio, originally from Ghana, immediately warmed to me and called me Uncle Joe (Tio Zé). I am happy to report that CEB's and Liberation Theology were high on his list of priorities and have been reinstated.

However, as one problem is solved, another is created. I was to be transferred back to the parish of St Marcos where I had first served as a priest in Sao Paulo, before going to Santarém. I would be able to continue my health projects as well as my duties as a priest, and I was delighted, but an even deadlier challenge was about to hit Brazil. It was the coronavirus. With all the religious power of prayer, and with all the healing properties of plants, this toxic infection, was about to inflict great suffering on the people, particularly the poor, the sick and the carers, who were most vulnerable as it was passed from one to the other. We all held our breaths as on the one hand we were advised by the health authorities to stay away from work, not to attend mass, and to self-isolate, while on the other hand, President Bolsonaro advised everyone to continue working, to treat it as normal, and let the strongest survive. We watched from our TV screens as Europe, Asia, Africa, Australasia, and the USA imposed lockdowns, and as the death figures rose higher and higher in Brazil, we buried our heads in shame.

CHAPTER 30

That's All I'll Need

The great challenge that Covid 19 posed for Brazil was the Government's inactivity and for the people to find ways to protect the poorest and most vulnerable. The parish united in force with the groups of JUPIC, Caritas de Sao Paulo, and the youth groups of Moises Liberator. Food packages and community soup kitchens were set up for those who lost their wages when places closed. Indeed, food was one of the most urgent needs. This was decided in the security council meetings in our neighbourhood. Normally the issues on the agenda were noisy funk street parties, motorbikes that revved up their engines on Sunday afternoons or robberies and fights. Sometimes specific policeman would be praised but these were rare. Now these issues were almost forgotten as the urgency of providing food to the neediest took priority.

From March 2020 all my health projects were cancelled and the Church began to place restrictions on liturgical celebrations. I twisted my ankle and at the same time, Norberto returned from Rondônia with a plan to have our masses live-streamed on You Tube and Facebook. On Palm Sunday, Norberto and a fellow priest celebrated mass in two communities with about six people present and the priests in tunics and stoles, walked the streets, blessing the palm branches of people in their homes, keeping a safe distance as recommended by the Ministry of Health.

On Easter Sunday, Pope Francis gave his Urbi and Orbi blessing to an empty St Peter's Square. Images of a cloudy sky and a pope alone, praying on a platform lit by the dim light of six candelabras reinforced the seriousness of the pandemic. "It's been night for weeks," he said, "Thick darkness has gathered over our squares, streets and cities; it has taken over our lives. The pandemic reminds us that we are all in the same boat……the storm exposes our vulnerability and uncovers the false and superfluous certainties around which we build our daily agendas…….we find ourselves afraid and lost. And now that we are in a stormy sea, we beg you: wake up Lord!"

But at least by staying at home, I found that it was an opportunity to catch up on reading, writing letters and listening to music like Teleman, Bach, Beethoven and Mozart. I was convinced too that it is providential that I slipped and twisted my ankle as I remembered the words of my first Health Guru, Yom Suk Yung, who said that when you hurt your feet, take them off the ground. Do not walk! So while I applied clay and took anti-inflammatories, I felt calmed.

I had lost the urgency to always be doing something. I continued to be appalled at Brazil's former president who promoted the use of chloroquine, a treatment for malaria, as Donald Trump had done, when there was no medical evidence to support that it eliminated the virus. When asked to comment on the 5000 deaths by Covid, he said: "So what! I'm sorry. What do you want me to do? I am Jair Messiah Bolsonaro, but I don't do miracles." At the end of 2021, Brazil had a total of 695,000 deaths from the Coronavirus and more than 36 million positive cases.

Contrary to Bolsonaro's unfeeling attitude, Pope Francis took a compassionate approach when he spoke of the number of deaths in Europe, the USA and across the world. There were times when there was no end in sight. It was a Cross that God had given us and we had to accept it. Our live-streamed masses were being followed each week by more than 200 people and there were perhaps only 6 – 9 people attending in person. We were all wearing masks when going out for essentials and as one person said, "I never thought the day would come when I could go into the bank masked and withdraw money!" But the disease continued to spread and killed the elderly and most vulnerable. 76% of those killed were over 60 years of age and even young people and children died. However, during the quarantine restrictions the parish worked behind the scenes and donations of food increased and more and more people received lunches, especially residents with no income. Video conferencing, Zoom and WhatsApp calls were taking place and we really discovered the benefits of technology.

I kept in touch with my previous parishioners in Santarém, in the river communities and they spoke to me of the harm that Bolsonaro's government had inflicted on their lifestyle. I remembered my last visit in 2014 when I gasped at the beauty of the Arapiuns River when in the morning light, the waters appeared like a mirror. It was in 1983 I first went to this region, and thirty years later it brought back so many memories. In 1983 I went up this river as a novice, an adventurer, a missionary, full of gas and enthusiasm. I was forty years old and at the beginning of a new phase in my life. Now looking back, I didn't have that same energy, but I still had enthusiasm for the Kingdom. I remembered the problems the indigenous people were facing. By admitting they were indigenous, they could receive grants, but this also meant they had to give up their properties. If they decided to leave their birthplace and move into the cities, with the help of the funding, they lost their land and homes. This is still a problem for future leaders of Brazil to solve.

There was also a big problem with loggers. I witnessed piles and piles of logs, all ready to be taken to Santarém and Belém, by huge ferries or rafts that could only be reached during this time of the flood. It was sad to see this wood being taken because someone from somewhere was earning a lot of money, while those who lived in these lands earned nothing. They lost the trees that preserved their sustainability. The government executives naturally received bonuses as a reward for granting tree-felling licences. What a pity I reflected; this region still had so much beauty. As all the majestic trees are felled, there will soon be another Rondônia, where the destruction of the Amazonian Forest is almost total.

I remembered the faces of the indigenous children, beautiful faces with beautiful skin, eyes full of hope, despite bad teeth. This was a result of the high sugar intake in their diet caused by advertisers encouraging them to eat and drink cheap processed sweets and snacks instead of the natural home-grown produce. I remember seeing so many very young mothers, under the age of 15, early adolescents with shaved eyebrows replaced with fake ones, and using lipstick, unable to recognize their own beauty and wanting to be like actresses in the soap operas they watched on TV when the village engine was running.

I remembered the beautiful beaches although I missed seeing them during this, my last trip, which was during the flood season. I slept on the riverboat Verbita that was piloted by Nelson, a very capable navigator and a young priest who understood the problems of the people. We chatted into the small hours by candlelight, there was no electricity and no mobile phone connections. I slept in a hammock as I had done 30 years before, and I awakened to a beautiful morning. The waves were quite strong on the boat and the water spray entered because the windows were open, but Nelson was capable, and no one was scared. By 12 noon, as we were almost entering the Tapajós River, leaving behind the Arapiuns and Maró rivers, the sun was reaching its highest point. It was getting hot. We were passing the tip of Vila Franca where my boat, the Antonio Meroth had sunk in 1988. I still remember Padre Zezinho's vinyl LP records, floating in the water as the boat sank. Drifting further and further away, a bit like life, each experience lived, but drifting further and further into the past.

And just as I spent my last moments in Santarém, Covid too began to be contained, and slowly, with the aid of science and the vaccine, we gradually emerged from the crisis, stronger and with resiliency, ready to take on the future, no matter what we faced. There are wounds still to be healed, but just as President Bolsonaro is voted out, President Lula is ready to take office, in the very month I celebrate my Golden Jubilee and 50 years as a priest.

There is renewed hope in our planet, with Lula seeking to reverse much of the destruction of Brazil's natural resources. Pope Francis is on his side too, with his Laudato Si message to the planet. Finally, under Lula's leadership, there will be a Ministry for Indigenous People and a Ministry for Climate Change. Lula has taken up the challenge – so perhaps then my work is done......and if I no longer have the need for purpose, I can relax a bit. I have a vision of myself with a bike, a place by the sea, some books, a hammock and a lamp light at night...and that's all I'll need....

God Bless

APPENDIX

SVD: Divine Word Missionaries

SSpS: Sister Servants of the Holy Spirit

SSpSPA: Sisters of Perpetual Adoration

Liberation Theology: an approach that emphasises the liberation of the poor through the readings of the gospels in communities, leading to a more dignified and proactive way of life. Its trademark is the option for the poor to be liberated through the spirituality of Christ's teachings.

CEB: Basic Ecclesiastical Communities - a global organisation where all people, particularly the poor, play an active role in the creation of an improved and fairer society that campaign for better health care and social facilities. In Latin America, following Vatican II, they were often actioned by lay people who were successful in reaching parts of society that clergy had previously been unable to do. With the support of bishops, priests, and religious congregations, they gained momentum providing a 'new way for the Church'. They continue to be guided by the Spirit of the Council, more recently in Pope Francis's call for Synodality.

Catechesis: the instruction in faith through the sacraments; encountering Jesus as man, and understanding his humanity

Myers Briggs Assessment: Personality Test

Charismatic Movement: a form of worship that shared its roots in Pentecostalism from the USA in the 1960s. It emphasises the gifts of the Holy Spirit through prayerful singing and clapping in personal or corporate praise. The emotion generated in worship can be interpreted as the presence or action of the Holy Spirit.

Evangelicals: Many denominations of fundamental Protestants and Pentecostals who may support conservative right-wing policies in the USA and Latin America

JUPIC: A movement for Justice, Peace and Integrity of Creation

Other Titles from MMCR Publications

Highly Commended by Scottish Association of Writers

Featured at Scottish Parliament
Year of Stories 2022

Children's Fiction Age: 8 -12
Published: August 2022
ISBN Number: 978-1-7396638-0-3
Synopsis: Set on the island of Cumbrae on the Ayrshire coast in 1263. Moranna, a Scots girl, and Sten a young Danish boy living in the Viking encampment nearby, become friends. The impending Battle of Largs will decide their fate.

"An engrossing read and a fascinating story, told with heart."
Scottish Association of Writers

Semi-Biographical Memoir; Social History; Politics, Romance
Published 2019
ISBN Number: 978-1-5272438-3-5
Synopsis: Florrie grows up in Dublin at the turn of the 20th century. Her future is set out for her as the eldest daughter in a Catholic middle-class family. But will she marry with the sweetheart who adores her, or take the chance in working in a couturiers in a prestigious Glasgow salon?

Available on Amazon or direct through:
www.maura.mcrobbie.com